T0120804

ASSESSING CULTURAL INFLUENCES IN
WORSHIP

DR. TIMOTHY D. PRICE, III

WESTBOW
PRESS®
A DIVISION OF THOMAS NELSON
& ZONDERVAN

This book is a work of non-fiction. Unless otherwise noted, the author and the publisher make no explicit guarantees as to the accuracy of the information contained in this book and in some cases, names of people and places have been altered to protect their privacy.

WestBow Press books may be ordered through booksellers or by contacting:

WestBow Press
A Division of Thomas Nelson & Zondervan
1663 Liberty Drive
Bloomington, IN 47403
www.westbowpress.com
844-714-3454

Because of the dynamic nature of the Internet, any web addresses or links contained in this book may have changed since publication and may no longer be valid. The views expressed in this work are solely those of the author and do not necessarily reflect the views of the publisher, and the publisher hereby disclaims any responsibility for them.

Any people depicted in stock imagery provided by Getty Images are models, and such images are being used for illustrative purposes only. Certain stock imagery © Getty Images.

Scripture taken from the NEW AMERICAN STANDARD BIBLE®, Copyright © 1960,1962,1963,1968,1971,1972,1973,1975,1977,1995 by The Lockman Foundation. Used by permission. www.Lockman.org

ISBN: 978-1-6642-0386-0 (sc)
ISBN: 978-1-6642-0387-7 (e)

Print information available on the last page.

WestBow Press rev. date: 9/24/2020

Assessing Cultural Influences in Worship

A Ministry Project Submitted to
the Faculty of the College of Theology
in Candidacy for the Degree of
Doctor of Ministry

by

Timothy D. Price, III

APPROVAL:

Chris Paris
Christopher Paris, PhD
Advisor

Scott E. McClelland

Scott E. McClelland, PhD
Chair, Department of Theology

Stephen Patton
Stephen Patton, DMin
Final Second

Christopher Porter
Christopher Porter, PhD
Reader Content/Style Reader

South University, Online
Date: November 2019

iii

CONTENTS

TABLES

ABSTRACT

Thesis: Church of the Living God Temple #203 will have greater harmony and unity amongst the membership as it learns to appreciate the diverse cultural influences that will be incorporated in its worship experience.

SUMMARY

The ministry setting for this project is a study in the life of Church of the Living God. The ministry setting of Church of the Living God is a blend of traditional and contemporary worship. Leaning more toward a traditional style of worship. This writer maintains that as society and culture evolve outside the church, so should the worship inside the church. Many congregations in the universal church have been attempting to transition their current worship styles. However, instead of maintaining an even blend of worship, they have been committing *syncretism* without an awareness of the difference. Therefore, a potential area of concern is to find what is missing in the elements of music and worship in the Church of the Living God and remain *authentic* yet *relevant*. This project will assess the chosen ministry setting, its current worship format, the music presented in it, and present a project to enhance the worship in the church.

To facilitate this, a representative group of a minimum of 30 individuals from the membership will be given a pre-survey to see what styles of music is desired and what they feel is appropriate for worship. From that group, a diverse smaller group of about 15-20 members will be picked based off the surveys to go through a "music appreciation course." This course will last for a minimum of four sessions. This course will expose them to a diversity of styles and advocates of those styles which are designed to also be worshipful. Once that is complete, a new survey will be completed. The intent is to show that change and unity was promoted, possible, and fruitful in this otherwise potentially divisive area of worship music. From the findings, focus will be placed on implementation. This will be presented by compiling a proposal to the pastor and church leadership to consider a more culturally inclusive style of worship.

This project will communicate how the influences of culture do not have to be a negative, but a positive influence when properly implemented in a worship setting. This will further show the importance that tangible investments in the worship format of the church will influence growth, expansion, community involvement, and *new conversion growth*. The conclusive intent from this project is to facilitate greater harmony between evolving generations in worship experiences and to make the worship at the Church of the Living God an inclusive experience.

ACKNOWLEDGEMENTS

Thank you, God for your Amazing Grace! I am because of You! Thank you to my wife (Kelli), and my children (Timothy, IV, Chrystopher, Lauren, Zoie, Lailah, Monjae, and Dalani) for dealing with me during this journey. It has been an extreme level of sacrifice for everyone. It has not been perfect, but God is getting the glory in the end. I pray that I made you all proud. I thank God for my mother who always pushed and supported my dreams. To my encouraging mother-in-law. Thank you! I have three siblings. We are all different, but we love each other. (Terrance, Raymond, and Jazzmine) To my extended family, friends, the pastors I have served, church family, fellow employees, mentors, churches, and organizations that have been influential to me throughout my journey.

This program would not have taken place without Church of the Living God, Temple #203 and Bishop Rex Waddell. Thank you for being my mentor and allowing me to use your church as a template for greater works in the kingdom. I pray that it made an impact on your local and national fellowship. Dr. F. James Clark for allowing me to bounce this topic off to him when I began this project and for being an advocate for me to push past my stopping points. Dr. Jaron Green, Dr. Terrence Hayes, and Bishop Shawn Bell are all men that I admire and look up too academically, spiritually, and personally.

Pastor Edgar Madison, Jr. you have been a mentoring force in my life all of my life. Thank you for never giving up on me. Bishop Shelton Bady thank you! As I continue to flourish and serve in the kingdom, I pray that I make you proud. Andrea Hayes, thank you for unselfishly helping me put this together when I was exhausted, and you were healing.

I am grateful for the entire faculty of Liberty University School of Music and South University School of Religion for excellent instruction and foundation given to me through my academic journey. Dr. Scott McClelland, Dr. Christopher Paris, Dr. Wayne Strickland at South University in particular, I have to thank you for pushing the best out of me during this program and final project. It has sharpened my thinking as you have coached me to the finish line.

Serving is my heart. It is a wonderful calling that God has created me to do. As I continue to position myself to make greater strides to serve the kingdom, I have to thank God for the village of people that have been my Healing Place. If I begin name any more names, it would take another page. You know who you are. It is my hope that my life and service to the kingdom will bring individuals closer to God and that churches will begin to flourish because of the access given from this project to become a more culturally inclusive place of worship.

FOREWORD

By Dr. Leo H. Davis, Jr.
Minister of Worship
Mississippi Boulevard Christian
Church "The Blvd"

Dr. Timothy D. Price, III shares insights and experiences, from over 30 years in music ministry, in a conversational manner that will appeal to those contemplating, beginning or fully invested in ministry. He gives intentional focus upon how music ministers should glorify God by finding multiple ways to meet the needs of humanity in worship. In particular, Dr. Price gives priceless nuggets on how the influences of culture can positively affect our worship experiences. In particular, how to properly facilitate greater harmony between evolving generations while obtaining the goal of inclusivity and unity. A must-read for every person involved in church music ministry.

CHAPTER ONE

Introduction

In the Christian Church, worship and music have evolved and will continue to do so over time. Music in worship serves as a useful tool to connect diverse groups of people with Christ. It sets the tone for obedience and needs being met in the atmosphere of worship. Therefore, the music presented in worship must reflect a generational balance with cultural significance so that the needs in worship are met for all individuals.

It is necessary that assessments and continuous changes are made in music for worship. It is a tune-up that must never be overlooked. As the needs of humanity evolve in worship, so must there be intentional progression of music in the worship life of the church. All music does not speak to the needs of every culture and generation. Improper practices of music in worship over time have caused tension and anxiety in the church. The choice of musical style has been the primary agitator of tension behind the scenes in the life of churches.

Every church culture has its own musical and liturgical style in worship. However, the exclusivity of musical styles in worship often separates generations. Music in worship must be an inclusive experience for all Christians in the church. To be inclusive suggests that no one particular group is the central focus in worship. Everyone is considered and balance is evident by the selections of music presented in worship. Exclusion is the opposite of inclusion. Exclusion separates and segregates generations, members, and cultures in the Christian Church.

Exclusion is not unfamiliar in the Christian Church. Many doctrines of the Christian Church focus on being "set apart" or isolated from the essence of the world and cultural elements that do not marry into the life of the Christian believer. Scripture says, "therefore, come out from their midst and be separate," says the Lord (2 Cor 6:17).[1] I have heard this scripture used many times in the church as a means of justification why certain methods and innovations should not be used in worship.

A part of my faith journey includes a doctrine that we must not have fellowship with unbelievers or the things that reflect the world. This belief formulated strong theological convictions as an individual, institution, community, and denomination. As a minister and leader in the Lord's Church, I championed this theology. However, I have grown to learn that this scripture has a much wider application to it. I always wondered why many local Pentecostal churches, which are a part of my faith heritage, never experienced exponential growth and were struggling.

As critical as it is for believers not to reflect the world, I wholeheartedly believe that task should not be difficult to accomplish. Scripture records that we "are a chosen race, a royal priesthood, a holy nation, a people for God's own possession, so that you may proclaim the excellencies of Him who has called you out of darkness into His marvelous light" (1 Pet 2:9). Believers reflect God's mercy, His grace, a regeneration, and a belonging to God that sticks out and separates believers from unbelievers.[2] Believers stick out in a way that can be infectious, attractive, and magnetic to unbelievers.

Without any changes in worship, it will be continuously

---

[1] All scripture will be New American Standard Bible version unless otherwise noted.

[2] Matthew Henry, *Matthew Henry Commentary on the Whole Bible* (Peabody, MA: Hendrickson Publishers, 2009), 1 Peter 2:9.

difficult for churches to see potential growth in the local church. I am convinced that the growing epidemic in the universal church is more than an issue of the times. People have not decided to not go to church because they do not need it. On the contrary, it is after careful examination, questions, and research that it has become increasingly clear to me that worship is one of the major contributors to the decline in the universal Christian church. Conservative churches are decreasing while the contemporary ones are increasing. People want to experience a worship that connects the dots in their life. Who they are genuinely and authentically in life and culture is how they are connected with God.[3]

I did some personal inquiries for answers from four of my colleagues who are pastors and leaders in local churches concerning this issue as I prepared for this project. From those inquiries, concrete answers were never obtained how to handle this protruding issue in the local church. Not only was music a major contributor to this issue, but greed, jealousy, self-serving spirits, independence, isolation, and refusal to learn were hindering forces behind this issue.[4] In many instances, leaders have simply succumbed to this epidemic with no plans to make changes.

Target Audience and Location of Ministry Setting

Unfortunately, I was not able to focus this project upon multiple churches. Therefore, I targeted only one church. That church was The Church of the Living God, Temple #203 in Fairview Heights, Illinois. Bishop Rex Waddell is the Senior Pastor of this local church. Church of the Living God, Temple #203 is a non-denominational church

---

[3] Dan Lucarini, *Why I Left the Contemporary Christian Music Movement: Confessions of a Former Worship Leader* (Darlington, England: Evangelical Press, 2002), 2.

[4] Vernon Whaley, "Building a Balanced Worship Ministry," *WRSP 551 Session 1: Liberty University.* Lecture, June 13, 2016.

that is a part of a fellowship of churches also known as Temples with numbers assigned to them.

This particular temple is 81years old. The current median age of the worshipers in this congregation are in their mid-50's and above. This age group is also named the Baby Boomers and Generation X. Currently the worship in Temple #203 is more exclusive to these particular generations rather than inclusive to all generations. However, there are other generations that must not be overlooked.

My plan and desire for this project is to hold on to the present generations while reaching for the generations that are not present in the church. This project targets the Baby Boomers, Generation X, Millennials, and other post generations. During this project, we will find effective styles of music that will encourage new conversion, growth, and a healthy direction for this church.

There will be individuals invited to volunteer their time for this project. All of them are members of this church. They will be the learning community for this project. Their mutual interest, passion for their church, and participation will enrich the information needed to fulfill the goals of this final project. The size of this group is small to give everyone opportunity to share their individual perspectives and that their voice will be heard. The climate and dynamic are very important for this project. It is essential that everyone feels free to express themselves in this journey of worship.

SPECIFIC MINISTRY NEED

One of the noticeable elements in the worship of Temple #203 is that the musical style has not been completely defined. They have a traditional style of musical choice in worship with a trace of contemporary. However, because the musical choice is not specific, I felt that I needed to find what are the missing pieces in the worship of this local church. Some of those missing pieces include lack of leadership and the lack of response to the reality that there are changes needed.

There are emerging cultures and generations at war between

the traditional and contemporary styles of worship. Change is constant, but the circumstances of change differ from generation to generation.[5] Each generation has a need and must feel free to express their love for God in their own way. As I have stated before, music and culture are constantly changing around us. It is necessary that the music in the local church remain fresh, reflect his glory in this age, and unify generations through the gospel.

Although things are changing in culture, one of the specific areas of need center around a lack of resources. However, scripture records that David did not have all of the resources and creative elements that we see in this modern age in worship. He simply had a harp and his heart sought to glorify God. "David would take the harp and play it with his hand," (1 Sam 16:23). He gave what he had, and God received it as an offering to bring Him glory. A simple use of a harp may not be as attractive in modern culture where technology and excitement are appealing. My goal for Temple #203 is to bring enlightenment on the possibilities in worship rather than the insufficiencies they have in the church.

IMPORTANCE OF THE TOPIC

This topic has increasingly become an important issue in the local and universal church. The topic of this project will provide a landscape to build a successful and inclusive worship experience for Temple #203. What will be extracted from this project will serve as a portal for growth and change. Otherwise, I believe that this church will be left behind from all of the other emerging churches and will continue to experience decline.

All music in worship should be relatable and influence an authentic experience with God. Otherwise, the lives in the church will become degenerate, shallow, selfish, and filled with humanistic

---

[5] Vernon M Whaley, *Called to Worship: From the Dawn of Creation to the Final Amen* (Nashville, TN: Thomas Nelson, 2009), xiii.

pursuits that do not glorify God.[6] The right music with the right heart will create an excitement and joy in the house of God according to Psalm 122:1. That same excitement will flourish and cause a spiritual overflow and exponential growth numerically, spiritually, and financially.

Thesis Statement

The purpose of this project was to offer a life-changing application and transformational journey in an area that has been historically divisive and contentious in the Christian Church. Substantial research, interviews, findings, education, and considerable analysis all contributed to the creation of this project. These foundations provided clarity and guidance for building a successful worship format that will include appropriate musical style choice for the generations present and forth coming. Church of the Living God Temple #203 will have greater harmony and unity amongst the membership as it learns to appreciate the diverse cultural influences that will be incorporated into its worship experience.

Personal Interest in the Topic

I personally have found myself drawn to this topic for several reasons. I have served in the area of worship and music for over 30 years and have seen multiple generations worshipping God together. I know that it is possible because I have experienced it before. Also, academically, I earned a Bachelor's degree which has an emphasis on Worship and my Master's degree specifically is in Worship.

As worship continues to evolve, it is very important to me that this topic needs to be brought to the forefront. This project

[6] David Wheeler and Vernon M. Whaley, *The Great Commission to Worship: Biblical Principles for Worship-Based Evangelism* (Nashville, TN: B & H Publishing Group, 2011), 116.

is the answer to much of the tension, anxiety, conflict, and decline in worship gatherings of the local church and community. I have lamented long enough over churches that show no signs of becoming culturally or generationally conscious in worship. These same churches are declining and struggling to survive. I have developed a burning passion for this topic and to create this project. It will serve as a bridge between all generations, churches, and communities by promoting change and establishing an inclusive worship experience.

OVERVIEW OF THE CONTENT OF THE MINISTRY PROJECT

An exhaustive analysis of this ministry setting was done prior to the actual implementation of this project. I collected a lot of information during several private meetings with the Senior Pastor of the ministry setting. I also spent hundreds of hours researching this topic. A pre- and post-survey was handed out to be completed by the volunteers that attended the seminar. The groundwork of this project was conducted in group discussions during four-week sessions of the Music and Worship Appreciation Seminar.

I am grateful that each level academically and spiritually has led me to this final place in my academic career. I had an educational plan for myself. Education has afforded me structure and space for growth.[7] To see that it coming to a final climax is breathtaking and overwhelming. I am excited about the hard work done and am looking forward to the results.

I have a short timeline at the ministry setting to complete this project. Time was of the essence. Therefore, I presented this topic and project in a way where follow up is necessary and encouraged. This project will be a template for this local ministry and the universal church at large in an evolving culture. I anticipate measurable

---

[7] Week 10: *"Rule of Faith or Life: Then and Now"* (online assignment introduction, MIN7050 Christian Spiritual Formation, South University), accessed May 4, 2018.

improvement, growth, and internal changes in this church. The volunteers for this project will be exposed too and educated of the multiple options they can have in worship. Transformative change will be unveiled and a new landscape in worship for the church will be discovered.

CHAPTER TWO

Community and Church Context

In order to lead and serve successfully in the context of worship, knowledge of the demographics and local trends surrounding the church is essential. This information enables leadership to become relevant in their ministry setting and community. From the research done for this ministry project, it has become clear to me that there are many churches struggling to be effectively relevant with their worship music. However, in order to be musically relevant, it is essential that leadership have an understanding of who and how to be relevant to the people they are serving by recognizing different age demographics as well as musical preferences and preconceived ideas about worship.

Community is an important dynamic found in Scripture. One passage says, "Behold, how good and how pleasant it is for brothers to dwell together in unity," (Ps 133:1). God's heart and desire is for humanity to live a life of relationship with Him and neighbors. In community, individuals are afforded opportunity to be vulnerable with God and each other. However, it is necessary in community that everyone feel comfortable in an environment that is relevant to their needs. Worship is one of those environments. Individuals are able to commune with God and each other during worship gatherings and small group settings.

During relevant worship experiences, individuals find strength and encouragement. John Donne said, "No man is an island entire of itself; every man is a piece of the continent, a part of the main…"[8] What Donne means by that statement is isolation and loneliness do not have to be an option. Icenogle said, "God beckons us into the presence of divine and human persons and relationships."[9] This is His covenant and will since creation.

The following information provides current and important demographics for the ministry setting of my ministry project and the community where they are planted. A concise description of the socioeconomic factors, ethnicities, religious affiliations, educational makeup, and the cultural influences in the church and community are provided throughout this chapter.

TABLE 2.1 SURVEY OF DEMOGRAPHICS IN THE COMMUNITY SURROUNDING THE MINISTRY SETTING

RACE/ETHNICITY

Caucasian	61.3%
Black	28.6%
Hispanic	2.7%
Asian	3.6%
Other	3.0%

GENDER

Males	46.8% = 7,901
Females	53.2% - 9,000

AGE
The median age of residents is 41 years old.

---

[8] John Donne. "XVII. Meditation." In *Devotions upon Emergent Occasions*, 108.

[9] Gareth Weldon Icneogle *Biblical foundations for Small Group Ministry: An Integrational Approach* (Downers Grove, IL: IVP, 1994), chp 5.

CRIME RATE
Below the national average per 100,000 people.

INCOME LEVEL PER HOUSEHOLD (DEFINE LOCAL DATA INCOME RANGES)
Estimated median household income is $62,489. (2016)

EDUCATION LEVELS

HS/GED	92.4%
Bachelors	31.8%
Graduate or Professional	14.5%

RELATIONSHIP STATUS

Never Married	31.6%
Now Married	49.1%
Separated	2.7%
Widowed	5.7%
Divorced	10.9%

FAITH TRADITIONS BEYOND CHRISTIANITY

Catholic	17.2%
Evangelical Protestant	17.4%
Orthodox	.8%
Black Protestant	3.8%
Mainline Protestant	9.1%
Other	2.2%
None	49.6%

The findings from the surveys done above are important to the development of my ministry project. They provide a broader scope of the community where the ministry setting is planted so that the church and community can seek innovations that will be more relevant in the ministry of the church and in worship. Soong Chan Rah concluded that there has always been a divide and disconnect between races, generations, and cultures.[10] However, in order to be effective in worship it is important to have insight to glean from. Further explanation of these findings and how they relate to this ministry project and ministry setting are shared in the next couple of sections.

RACIAL AND ETHNIC MAKE-UP
OF ATTENDEES IN WORSHIP

The congregation of Temple #203 is 99.9% African American. The majority race in that community is Caucasian. I do not feel that there should be an issue with Temple #203 because it is a predominantly black church. As a matter of fact, Sallie McFague stated that "human beings are individuals motivated by self-interests."[11] What she means is we connect with people that look more like us and have similar backgrounds.

The surveys show that Temple #203 has become an isolated church in a community that is predominately Caucasian for African Americans. This limits any ethnic possibilities of growth and outreach in the community where they are planted. Therefore, diversity will have to be seen and promoted in other areas that do not include ethnicity in order to see growth numerically. Allan Johnson said, "unless you live in a culture that recognizes such differences (as race) as significant, they are socially irrelevant and therefore, in a way, do not exist."[12] We do not choose what race we are, but we do choose where we worship and with whom we worship.

---

[10] Soong Chan Rah, *Many Colors: Cultural Intelligence for a Changing Church* (Chicago: Moody Publishers, 2010), 52.

[11] Sallie McFague. *Life Abundant: Rethinking Theology and Economy for a Planet in Peril.* (Minneapolis, MN: Fortress Press, 2001), 75.

[12] Week 5: "*Race Matters*" (online assignment introduction, MIN7060 Diversity in Ministry, South University), accessed August 27, 2017.

EDUCATION LEVEL OF ATTENDEES IN WORSHIP

Another area that should be assessed is the education level of the attendees in the church. From my personal assessment, I was able to see that education is a high priority to Bishop Waddell and in the life of Temple #203. During my conversations with Bishop Waddell, he shared with me that he is working on his doctoral degree in Education. His pursuit of higher education influences him to encourage the members of his congregation to do the same. Several of the outreach programs started under his leadership center around education.

Some of those outreach programs include Project Positive Force, which is a community development program that gives awards to the top five students with the highest-grade point average each quarter. 92.4% of the population in the community have at least a high school diploma and 31.8% have an undergrad degree. The educational demographic in the church and the priority leadership has shown is something that can be built upon and expanded in the community. Developing a culture of learning and educational values for leaders of worship and the congregation will create greater opportunities in worship. John Fitzgerald Kennedy said, "Leadership and learning are indefensible to each other."[13]

CULTURAL INFLUENCES

Cultural influences are also significant because they influence politics, society, worship, behaviors, and the way of life. In most cases, culture has nothing to do with biblical application. However, cultural influences have become common in the church. Influences such as place, time, attire, style, and customs that have been implemented in worship.

Jesus was aware of the cultural norms in society when he

---

[13] "JFK Library." Remarks Prepared for Delivery at the Trade Mart in Dallas, TX, November 22, 1963. Accessed May 16, 2019. https://www.jfklibrary.org/.

ministered to individuals and communities. This is why He transcended beyond the many different cultures and embodied a Gospel that has a remarkable record of crossing vast cultural divides.[14] He surpassed culture, but He did not ignore it.

Culture influences promote authentic and genuine worship. The many languages, races, rituals, and diversity in society is a reality that cannot be ignored. All of these contribute to the process and journey of worship. According to the Nairobi Statement on Worship and Culture, worship has related dynamically to culture in four ways.

- Trans-cultural: the same for everyone, everywhere, and goes beyond culture
- Contextual: it varies to the local culture and nature
- Counter-cultural: Biblical principle challenges what is in that culture
- Cross-cultural: different local cultures share[15]

Jesus was born into Jewish culture. He worshipped God according to His culture. In the mystery of his incarnation, there is a mandate for contextualization of Christian worship.[16] In a world filled with diversity, contextualization is necessary for the church. The adaption and influence of culture should not erase critical and basic elements of the Gospel when the focus and passion of worship is to meet the needs of the local culture of the people.

From further research and assessments, I have seen churches trying to meet the needs of the evolving and coming generations but failing horribly. Many would argue with my assessment; however, the proof is in the stagnation of growth in the majority of churches in our communities. Focus has been placed upon relevancy by adapting to culture and trying to exclude important religious elements in

---

[14] Charles E. Farhadian, *Christian Worship Worldwide: Expanding Horizons, Deepening Practices* (Grand Rapids, MI: Eerdman Publishing, 2007.), 275.

[15] Ibid, 285.

[16] Ibid, 287.

worship. Warren Bird wrote, "Our failure to impact contemporary culture is not because we have not been relevant enough, but because we have not been real enough."

The relevancy of worship must promote "spiritual health but cannot if it has become diseased with separatism whether stated or functional."[17] Every generation desire to feel that their needs are important and that they are effectively being served in worship. No generation wants to feel undervalued, unappreciated, irrelevant, and unimportant.[18] For clarity, below is an outline of the different generations in society:

> The Silent Generation: Born 1925 – 1945
> Baby Boomer Generation: Born 1946 – 1964
> Generation X (Baby Bust): Born 1965 – 1979
> Millennials: Born 1980 - 1994
> iGen/Gen Z: Born 1995 – 2012
> Gen Alpha: Born 2013 - 2025[19]

It would be beneficial for Temple #203 to have an understanding of each generation that is present in the church and the ones that are not. The majority population in Temple #203 are the Baby Boomers and Generation X.[20] This shows that there is a disproportion and absence of Millennials and other post generations. Temple #203 would benefit from the participation and presence of those underserved generations.

---

[17] Sally Morgenthaler, *Worship Evangelism: Inviting Unbelievers into the Presence of God* (Grand Rapids, MI: Zondervan, 1999), 30.

[18] Week 7: *"Bridging Generational Differences"* (online assignment introduction, MIN7060 Diversity in Ministry, South University), accessed September 12, 2017.

[19] Michael T. Robinson, and CareerPlanner.com. "The Generations - Which Generation Are You?" Which Generation Are You? Last accessed on January 05, 2019 from http://www.careerplanner.com/

[20] Rex Waddell (Ministry Assessment), interviewed by Timothy Price, III, Fairview Heights, IL, May 23, 2018.

SUBCULTURAL INFLUENCES

Subculture influences are typically facilitated by smaller groups within the larger scheme of culture. These subcultures can be politically, racially, and even morally motivated. The challenge with subculture is it can have an effect upon true and authentic worship. In the Old Testament, there were subcultures. They worshipped in a manner in which the Bible calls it *true, vain, or false worship.* For example:

1. **The people of Israel and the golden calf** – They worshipped in the wrong way. This is also known as false worship. The people of Israel became anxious and inpatient while they were waiting for Moses to come down from the mountain. Therefore, they chose to make their own god in the form of a golden calf. They were ultimately punished by a plague for their disobedience (Exod 32). This idolatry returned later in Israel's history. During the era of the Divided Kingdom, the northern kingdom of Israel worshiped calves in Dan and Bethel instead of at the true place of worship in Jerusalem.

2. **Nadab and Abihu** – They worshipped the right God but in the wrong way. This is act is known as vain worship. They worshipped the Lord by burning strange fire which was the opposite of what the Lord commanded. They were punished and died in the presence of the Lord (Lev 10).

3. **King Uzziah** – He worshipped the right God in the right way. This act is known as true worship. He did what was right in the sight of the Lord. The result of his worship was he was blessed with longevity, his days were prosperous, and God gave him revelation (2 Chr 26).

CULTURAL INFLUENCES FROM THE BIBLE

Despite what culture one may be from, there is a commonality as it relates to worship. That commonality is the desire to worship. The Bible has influenced culture in and out of the church. Jesus made it clear to the woman at the well by telling her that she will no longer worship in the way it was in the Old Testament. The Old Testament ways of worship was filled with rituals, sacrifices, festivals, and institutions established for worship. All of these were established in order to create a holy place for the presence of God to be experienced by man.

For example, when Jesus had his conversation with the woman at the well, He pointed out to her that neither time, place, culture, nor tradition will restrict our individual or corporate worship. "Jesus said to her, "Woman, believe Me, an hour is coming when neither in this mountain nor in Jerusalem will you worship the Father. You worship what you do not know; we worship what we know, for salvation is from the Jews. But an hour is coming, and now is, when the true worshipers will worship the Father in spirit and truth; for such people the Father seeks to be His worshipers. God is spirit, and those who worship Him must worship in spirit and truth" (John 4:21-24). The sacrifices of the Old Testament are no longer required as atonement for sin. Christ, the Lamb of God, was the ultimate sacrifice and prepared the way and enabled for this to come to pass.

King David is known for his praise and worship. He influenced music, instrumentation, and songs in scripture. Congregational worship, entering with thanksgiving, non-sacrificial worship, the use of the guitar, dancing, and sacrificial offerings have all been influenced by David in church culture. These are a few contributions to the storyline of worship in the Old Testament.

In scripture, established places for worship were synagogues, tabernacles, temples, and churches. These places were holy places created so that God could dwell amongst mankind. However, they are no longer the only places where worship is facilitated. Mankind now has unlimited access to God through Jesus Christ. The relationship between God and man no longer has boundaries, restrictions, or restraints from the Old Testament traditions.

Jesus Christ is in the center of it all. Jesus came into the world as the conductor, directing the greatest symphony of harmony between God and man. His life produced a worship response that destroyed the powers of sin and death.[21] The story of worship cannot be complete without Jesus.

In the New Testament book of Acts, the coming of the Holy Spirit on the Day of Pentecost is one of the most notable times of worship. Every barrier was broken because of the power of the Holy Spirit. One of the most important and needed elements in worship today is the presence of the Holy Spirit. Scripture says, "When the day of Pentecost had come, they were all together in one place. And suddenly there came from heaven a noise like a violent rushing wind, and it filled the whole house where they were sitting. And there appeared to them tongues as of fire distributing themselves, and they rested on each one of them. And they were all filled with the Holy Spirit and began to speak with other tongues, as the Spirit was giving them utterance." (Acts 2:1-4) The presence of God creates an atmosphere for the confessions of man's faith, testimonials, congregational singing, singing of hymns and spiritual songs, preaching, laying hands on the sick, and freedom of expression through worship.

The information from this chapter helps to facilitate a gateway of opportunity for this ministry project and the worship ministry of Temple #203. The influence of culture is not a new phenomenon. It dates back to biblical times. This chapter helps Temple #203 develop a more conscientious way to adapt to the cultural changes through methodical changes while fulfilling the mission and purpose of the church.

The ministry project that is developed for Temple #203 is centered on preparation, planning, and a call to action for the needed changes in worship. Worship builds people, churches, and communities. This should be an unconditional commitment in the life of any ministry setting and in the larger Christian community. "The Lord is not slow about His promise, as some count slowness, but is patient toward you, not wishing for any to perish but for all to come to repentance," (2 Pet 3:9). This is His will and the fruit of worship.

---

[21] Robert E. Webber, *Worship Old and New* (Grand Rapids, MI: Zondervan, 1994), 41.

ANALYSIS OF THE MINISTRY SETTING

MISSION AND HISTORY OF THE CHURCH OF THE LIVING GOD

The ministry setting for this ministry project is the Church of the Living God (COTLG). The COTLG Brotherhood, Christian Workers for Fellowship was established in April 1889 about twenty-four years after the Emancipation Proclamation that called for the end of slavery. The founder of this non-denominational fellowship was Rev. William Christian, a Baptist Pastor from Arkansas. He preached the Gospel message of Jesus Christ. His desire to preach this message was met with challenges, hardship, and opposition from his counterparts in the Baptist church. Therefore, he left the Baptist Denomination and organized the Church of the Living God.

The COTLG proclaims to be a non-denominational and non-sectarian entity, which means it is not connected or involved with any formal or Christian denomination. However, the organizational structure that it has causes me to challenge that stance. According to Pamela Gentry, "a non-denominational church or organization chooses their own worship rituals, leadership structure, and how they govern themselves as Christians."[22]

COTLG is the oldest non-denominational church organization in the United States. The beliefs of this organization rest on being a Bible-believing, people loving, and a God serving nationally based church.[23] Elements that are a part of their worship practices include baptism by total immersion, the Lord's Supper with unleavened bread, and washing of feet when one unites with the church. These important practices are biblical expressions that are often used in

---

[22] Newsmax. "6 Non-Denominational Christian Churches and Organizations." Newsmax. April 22, 2015. Last accessed May 14, 2019 from https://www.newsmax.com/

[23] "Cotlgministries2018." Cotlgministries2018. Last accessed December 15, 2018 from https://www.cotlgministries.org

the context of their worship. They affect one's perception of Jesus and the church.[24]

The COTLG currently has 12 Episcopal Districts throughout the United States and Africa. The local churches are identified as a "Temples". In less than ten years after its inception, over sixty temples were established with approximately 853 members throughout the United States in Tennessee, Arkansas, Missouri, Mississippi, Texas, Kansas, Oklahoma, and Illinois. Churches are organized into districts.[25] Each district is presided over by a Bishop which provides leadership to all the temples in their assigned district.

The national organization is led by the elected Executive Presiding Bishop who is also known as the "Chief" Bishop along with an Executive Board of bishops. The local Temple a part of this organization that will be the ministry setting for my project is in Fairview Heights, Illinois. The church is known as The Church of the Living God, Temple #203. The Senior Pastor is Elder Rex Waddell. He was appointed the Senior Pastor of Temple #203 in 1989. In 2018, he was elected as the "Chief Bishop" for the Church of the Living God C.W.F.F. organization nationally.

Temple #203 was organized in 1938 in the city of East St. Louis by Elder Joseph Hopkins and his wife Etha Lee Hopkins. The mission and purpose of the church is to lead others in becoming fully devoted disciples of Jesus Christ. Under the current leadership of Bishop Waddell, he has continued that mission and purpose by teaching individual healthy lifestyles, providing and promoting academic, social academic opportunities, and social reformation that honors God and edifies humankind. He inspires the members in that local congregation to be innovative, relevant, inspiring, and encouraging so that mission and purpose of that local church will be fulfilled.

---

[24] Brad House, *Community: Taking Your Small Group Off Life Support* (Wheaton, IL: Crossway, 2011), 129.

[25] "Cotlgministries2018." Cotlgministries2018. Last accessed December 15, 2018 from https://www.cotlgministries.org.

RANGE OF MINISTRIES AND PROGRAMS

The mission and purpose of the church that is established by the Senior Pastor of the church sets the tone for what type of ministries and programs will aid in championing those goals. Bishop Waddell and I had a series of unofficial interviews where he gave me some vitals and his personal assessment as the Senior Pastor of the church. One of those areas of discussion focused on the ministries and programs that have been implemented in the life of the church. Those current ministries are:

1. Audio & Video – This ministry handles sound, board operations, and duplication machines for marketing and sales. This ministry does not require prior experience. Interested individuals are trained.

2. Greeters – Those in this ministry are responsible for assuring that every individual who enters the doors of the church are greeted with a warm welcome. Those serving in this ministry should be energetic, friendly, and have a love for people.

3. Health Services – This ministry embraces one of the pillars of the vision for the church which is to "promote healthy lifestyles." Health service attendants in this ministry do not have to be career health professionals. However, anyone interested in this ministry must be trained in order to serve.

4. School of the Kings – This ministry is also known as the "Men's Ministry." Facilitated through this ministry, men are provided with educational, emotional, and spiritual growth programs.

5. Women's Ministry – This ministry offers opportunity for women to grow and develop through prayer, fellowship, outings, biblically based instruction and mentoring.

6. Youth Ministry – This ministry has multiple areas which are continuously being designed to lead every child into becoming a devoted disciple of Jesus Christ.

7. M.A.N.N.A (Metro Area Necessary Nutritional Assistance) Food Pantry – This ministry is a mobile food pantry which serves over two hundred families monthly. This ministry is not limited to the Missionaries and Deacons.

8. CMC (Crossroads Multipurpose Center) – This facility is a newer addition to the church. It is a multipurpose facility used for weddings, parties, and other gatherings. Creating space and opportunity for those who are not members of COTLG to connect with the ministry in one way or another.

9. Music Ministry – This ministry is a vehicle for individuals to share their gifts in the worship gathering. They share the Gospel of Jesus Christ through song. This ministry includes: Youth Choir, Musicians, Adult Choir, Men's Choir, and Praise Team.

LEADERSHIP AND DECISION-MAKING PROFILE

It takes solid leadership to develop the programs and ministries listed above. Ministries serve as vehicles and or avenues to maximize growth, fellowship, education, and opportunity to share individual gifts in the church. Ministries help people feel that their lives matter. Therefore, ministries and programs must be shaped to meet needs of people who gather for worship and live in the community.

When leaders decide to organize certain ministries in the church, it is important that it serves a purpose. Most people that join a church desire to be a part of one that is meaningful, liberating, and personal. Therefore, the church and any ministry that operates under the umbrella of the church must focus on building great people.

Leaders have the ability to empower, influence, and create change in the community. I can point out a few leaders in scripture that are worth highlighting beginning with Jehoshaphat. He was a historical king in the Bible that successfully led the people of his community toward victory. Jehoshaphat was a great leader. However, his leadership revealed his humanity. Therefore, all of his decisions were not always the best or manifested victory.

In 1 Kings and 2 Chronicles, the political system of Jehoshaphat was characterized by the alliances that he made. He was considered to be of mature age and well trained when he became king. In 2 Chronicles 18, a major shift took place because of Jehoshaphat's decision as a leader. He married off his son Jehoram to Athaliah the daughter of Ahab who was the wicked king of Israel. This decision was made with the intent of building a political alliance with King Ahab. However, this alliance was already prophesied that this decision would have negative consequences. From this decision, the balance of power shifted to Israel from Judah's favor.

Israel became more powerful economically, politically, and in military. This decision became disastrous for Judah. It had rippling effects upon Jehoshaphat and the community he was leading. This is an example of how great leaders have the ability to make bad decisions. Our humanity can definitely influence our choices, oscillating between what is right and wrong.

The Apostle Paul wrote "I find then the principle that evil is present in me, the one who wants to do good. For I joyfully concur with the law of God in the inner man, but I see a different law in the members of my body, waging war against the law of my mind and making me a prisoner of the law of sin which is in my members." (Rom 7:21-23). Paul is saying that his mind is under attack, telling him one thing while his heart is saying another. This struggle can be burdensome on leaders who are trying to decide what is best for their church and community.

After the bad decisions of Jehoshaphat, he sought counsel from the Lord. He realized that any decision without God will potentially be disastrous. Jehoshaphat was an example of a leader who wrestled with his humanity but had a willingness to do right by and for the people he was serving. In other words, he was a great shepherd but not the best leader. Although he was warned and knew what he was supposed to do, his heart influenced final decision.

"We can choose to acknowledge our dark side, practice a life of transparency before God, and let down our guard, knowing that he will begin his refining and empowering work in us; or we can choose to live in denial and even masquerade before God, fueling the ongoing development of our dark side."[26] The lessons that can be gleaned from Jehoshaphat's leadership shows that that leaders are not born; they are made through hard work, discipline, and sacrifice.

Jehoshaphat was not perfect, but he was faithful. He was a spiritual leader whose humanity could not be ignored. The greatness of his leadership lied in his ability to be humble and willing to allow God to lead him even after he made some horrible decisions. He committed to walking with God even in the midst of difficulty. Although his life did not end in triumph, his heart was devoted to God. Leaders must always, "Trust in the Lord with all your heart and do not lean on your own understanding. In all your ways acknowledge Him, and He will make your paths straight." (Pro 3:5-6)

One more leader in scripture that revealed His humanity was Jesus Christ. One of those instances when he revealed that humanity was in Matthew 24:36. "But of that day and hour no one knows, not even the angels of heaven, nor the Son, but the Father alone." He expressed that he did not know everything. Only God did. They were drawn toward Him because His life and ministry exemplified authenticity, discipline, humility, and genuine concern to meet needs. What He taught, He also modeled. He asked the disciples to "Follow Me, and I will make you fishers of men," (Matt 4:19). What He modeled made the disciples open to following Him.

The purpose of sharing these two historic figures was to help to provide a clear picture that even the greatest leaders do not always have the answers to everything. Also, our humanity can get in the way of seeing what the best decision for the church and community of the ministry setting is.

After an extensive and transparent interview with Bishop Waddell, I was able to conclude that he was devoted to the things of God as a leader. He has experienced success and failure in ministry. During our interview, he was candid and honest with me concerning

---

[26] Gary McIntosh. *Overcoming the Dark Side of Leadership: How to Become an Effective Leader by Confronting.* (Grand Rapids, MI: Baker Books, 2007), 170.

the challenges he presently was facing as a and his desire to see revival to take place in his church and community.[27]

In many non-denominational churches, the pastor is the leading principal over all the decisions in the church. Everything that the pastor decides will affect the church and community. Therefore, it is expedient that he must lead with discernment knowing when to make the right move at the right moment with the right motives.[28] John Maxwell calls this leadership style the "lead down" principle. This principle says that one must model the behavior they desire to see in others. This leadership style determines the culture, sets the tone, pace, can create an environment of productivity, enthusiasm, trust, and growth.

The members are allowed to "exercise their right to think and choose"[29] concerning important matters of the church. However, they are influenced by their leader's values, work behavior, quirks, and habits. In the COTLG, the pastor interprets and helps the congregation understand what God is saying to the church, community, and how the work which God has called them to is done.[30] All final decisions completely rests upon the pastor. John Maxwell says, "If you don't like what your people are doing, first take a look at yourself.[31]

One of the most powerful contributions in any organization is what the leader does. Our choices greatly influence those we lead.

---

[27] Rex Waddell (Ministry Assessment), interviewed by Timothy Price, III, Fairview Heights, IL, May 23, 2018.

[28] John C. Maxwell, *The 360 Leader: Developing Your Influence from Anywhere in the Organization* (Nashville, TN: Thomas Nelson, 2011),139.

[29] Week 2: *"Acknowledging the Problem"* (online assignment introduction, MIN7160 Ministry in the Local Church, South University). Last accessed May 18, 2018.

[30] Week 2: *"Understanding Ordained and Lay Ministry"* (online assignment introduction, MIN7160 Ministry in the Local Church, South University), accessed May 18, 2018.

[31] John C. Maxwell, *The 360 Leader: Developing Your Influence from Anywhere in the Organization* (Nashville, TN: Thomas Nelson, 2011), 147.

If our decisions and choices are not making the difference, then it may be time for reinforcements, maybe even an alliance. When doing so, it is essential that who and what fall in line with our theological convictions, core values, mission, and purpose for ministry.

CORE VALUES AND THEOLOGICAL CONVICTIONS

The core values and theological convictions in most cases are influenced by religious leaders. Theology teaches about God's creation, the condition of man, and God's redemptive plan for all humanity.[32] Often what we believe about those things are inherited from a combination of scriptures, leaders, culture, church, and experience. The Bible is the heart of all Christian traditions. It is the divine answer to every human condition and is the inspired revelation of God.

In this present age and culture people are seeking to find God outside of religious expression and in a way that is not linked to the Bible. James Sawyer states that "theologians may feel free to explore other sources of potential interest; doctrine is historically linked with Scripture."[33] The Church has historically acted as an independent authority in theology. It "has been the independent authority to the members of churches by providing its own interpretive traditions and scripture" that create what one holds as truth as their system of values and faith.[34] Temple #203's theological conviction and Articles of Faith originated from the National Organization that they are a part of, which is cited at the end of this list. Below are the core values that give foundation for their theological convictions.

---

[32] Millard J. Erickson. *Christian Theology.* (Grand Rapids, MI: Baker Academic, 2013), 8.

[33] M. James Sawyer. *The Survivor's Guide to Theology.* 1st ed. (Grand Rapids, MI: Zondervan, 2006), 119.

[34] Ibid., 119.

"We believe in One true and Living God, the Creator of Heaven and Earth, and the Father of the Lord and Savior, Jesus Christ.

We believe there are three persons in the Godhead, namely: The Father, the Son, and the Holy Ghost.

We believe that Jesus Christ is the Redeemer of mankind.

We believe that Jesus died, was buried, arose, and ascended into heaven.

We believe Jesus Christ to be the door to Eternal Life and we are to enter into the City through and by Jesus Christ.

We believe that any attempt made to enter the fold of God without following Christ's instructions makes a complete failure and that one cometh before the Mighty One as a thief and a robber.

We believe there are three Sacraments ordained of Christ in the New Covenant, namely: Baptism, the Lord's Supper, and the Washing of Feet.

We believe in the Fatherhood of God and the Brotherhood of man.

We believe all are one in Christ, who does His will.

We believe we should do unto all men, as we would have them do unto us.

We believe all men are born free and equal.

We believe that the Holy Bible is the book, which points out the Way of eternal Life through obedience.

We believe to be saved, we must live by every word (pertaining to salvation) that proceedeth out of the mouth of God.

We believe the Bible from Genesis to Malachi to be a Jewish guide foreshadowing the coming of Christ.

We believe the Gospel recorded in Matthew, Luke, and John contains the plan of salvation.

We further believe that the book of Acts may be used as by-laws in part and as a history of the apostolic work.

We believe the book of Revelation was sent from God, signified by an angel unto John for inspiration and encouragement of the Disciples of Christ.

We believe all scripture is profitable for Doctrine, for reproof, for correction, and for instruction in righteousness, so that the man of God may be perfect, thoroughly furnished, unto all good works."[35]

These core values influence the standards set for living as well as what the church reveals about God through their religious practices. These theological convictions also provide relative interpretative traditions that are revealed in scripture.[36] It is the responsibility of

---

[35] "Church of The Living God C.W.F.F. National Brotherhood." Church of The Living God C.W.F.F. National Brotherhood. Accessed December 17, 2018 from http://www.ctlgcwff.org/

[36] M. James Sawyer, *The Survivor's Guide to Theology* 1st ed. (Grand Rapids, MI: Zondervan, 2006), 119.

worship leaders to ensure that inaccuracies are not presented in the music selected for worship. These core values also enlighten what is embraced during worship. Some of those are washing feet, the Lord's Supper, baptism, etc.

What we believe about God is revealed in the lyrics of songs. It is critical that appropriate songs are chosen for worship. For example, songs about the Holy Spirit would not be presented in worship if there was no belief in the Trinity or the Holy Spirit. Songs that support the core values of the church help to shape and enforce the values, beliefs, and faith.

OBSTACLES ASSOCIATED WITH THE MINISTRY PROBLEM

The core values help to narrow down confusion in a particular ministry setting. Adversity is easy to manifest when preparing and planning for worship. Restated, one of the areas that has proven to generate the greatest tension, anxiety, and conflict is worship.[37] It has the ability to weaken or strengthen the productivity of the church. Worship should be a continuous and evolving journey. However, when it stops evolving, the pressures of culture and people begin to scream for more. Screams that will continue and never disappear unless addressed and validated.

The mission of the universal church is to reconcile the world to God through Jesus Christ.[38] The tension that is experienced in the church has nothing to do with the mission. It is the methods of accomplishing it that must be evaluated. Worship is one of those areas of challenge and tension.

One of the most visible obstacles concerning worship at Temple #203 is that generations are being left out and segregated in worship.

---

[37] Robb Redman, *The Great Worship Awakening: Singing a New Song in the Postmodern Church* (San Francisco: Jossey-Bass, 2002.), xiii.

[38] Will McRaney, Jr., *Unceasing Worship: The Art of Personal Evangelism* (Nashville, TN: B & H Publishing, 2003), 16.

After visiting a couple worship services and a few interviews with Bishop Waddell, he shared with me that the median age in Temple #203 is 55 and up, which is around his age.[39] He concluded that after pastoring this same church for 30 years, the present state of the church is visibly aging and progressing in an unhealthy direction.[40] An unhealthy church is one where there is little to no statistical growth (numerical, spiritual, or otherwise) and minimal impact on the surrounding culture.[41] There are various areas where growth is necessary in order for the church to move in a "healthy direction."

There are many innovative expressions that can be done in the church to reach diverse people and to meet the needs of multiple generations. What was done yesterday may not be good for today or tomorrow. The norms and methods of yesterday have become obstacles and areas of contention that are ineffective and have become stale. This brings a greater value to the need for my ministry project. An important element of this ministry project are the surveys and discussions with the volunteers during the project. These couple of weeks allowed me to further hear the heart of the people and to see where the disconnect is. This will be discussed in further chapters that actually deal with the ministry project.

Knowing what God's best for the church requires education, sincere prayer, asking questions, assessment, and courage, the overall concept of worship must be a continuous and passionate pursuit between God and man that transcends time, place, culture, and any other obstacles or restrictions. One of the key things to moving past any obstacles is to address them. One of the greatest obstacles in any area of leadership that has seemingly hit a "brick wall" is denial that there is a problem. Leaders have become content with their past experiences and have lost the hunger for where they need to be

---

[39] Rex Waddell (Ministry Assessment), interviewed by Timothy Price, III, Fairview Heights, IL, May 23, 2018.

[40] Waddell.

[41] Warren Bird, Ed Stetzer, and Elmer Towns, *11 Innovations in the Local Church*. (Ventura, CA: Regal Books, 2007), 14.

going. They have chosen to refuse to embrace the realities of what is happening around them for the fear of losing their separateness from the world. The scripture that is often used to justify that mindset says, "'Therefore, come out from their midst and be separate,' says the Lord." (2 Cor 6:17).

There is a difference in being separate and isolated. This scripture is giving a call to believers. We must forsake the company and conversations of men and ways of the world after conversion. However, in order to accomplish the ministry and mission of God, we must promote a mission that goes beyond the church. The Word of God is not exclusive to only believers. Therefore, worship should not be only exclusive to certain generations, cultures, and people. It should be inclusive for everyone. Leaders who choose to isolate themselves from culture find their ministries becoming stagnant; they become discouraged, stressed, etc.

There are thousands of churches across the United States that vary in size. They range from "storefront" to "mega-size" facilities. In the mindset of some, they can be renamed as "successful" or "unsuccessful" churches. A declining church can bring about discouragement in the heart of a leader. This is a perception that must be managed. Otherwise, it will influence internal and external conflict in the leader and church because of skewed perceptions, fatigue, frustration, and fear. A sad reality is some leaders and churches have never bounced back from these obstacles.

Worship is a process that involves continuous planning, preparation, growth, maturity, courage, and spiritual formation individually and corporately. It also must be fluid yet maintain balance in an ever-changing culture and society. A few tangible ways to remedy these obstacles are:

1. Prayer must be a pillar and important discipline in the ministry.
2. Clear Mission Statements, Strategic Visions (5-year plan), Goals (3-5-year plan), Strategies (1-3-year plan), and Objectives. (1-year plan)

3. Share the vision and create a Solid Team.
4. Strong leadership builds strong ministry.

These are some overall solutions. However, when there is conflict in worship, it affects the heart of people. Greg Scheer said, "People today may differ about worship, but at least they care."[42] Worship matters in the heart of humanity. Real worship, among other things, is a feeling in the heart.[43] Therefore it is important to mankind how we think, respond, are changed, loved, and more when in worship. "God is a person, and in the deep of his mighty nature He thinks, wills, enjoys, feels, loves, desires, and suffers as any other person may."[44] Therefore, His heart cares how He is worshipped as much as man cares how they worship Him.

Matters of the heart create emotions of happiness and fulfillment when things go well. When worship does not go well, negative emotions arise. One of the most sensitive areas of discussion during the ministry project had to do with the music ministry and their lack of growth from a musical standpoint.[45] From this discussion, I concluded that there seems to be no clear vision or strong leadership for the music ministry. Conflict begins and ends with leadership.

According to *Christianity Today*, negative and positive outcomes manifest in conflict. Some of those negative outcomes include damaged relationships, sadness, decline in attendance, leaders vacating their position, loss of trust with members and community, and bitterness. There are also positive outcomes that can manifest from conflict. The pastor becomes wiser, purification, better

---

[42] Greg Scheer, *The Art of Worship: A Musician's Guide to Leading Modern Worship* (Grand Rapids, MI: Baker Books, 2006), 16.

[43] A.W. Tozer, *The Purpose of Man* (Ventura, CA: Regal from Gospel Light, 2009), 108.

[44] David Wheeler and Vernon Whaley *The Great Commission to Worship: Biblical Principles for Worship-Based Evangelism* (Nashville, TN: B & H Publishing, 2011), 96.

[45] Timothy Price, III. *Music Appreciation Course*. Fairview Heights, IL, 2018.

defined vision, stronger relationships, reconciliation, and growth in attendance: 15%.[46]

Conflict does not have to be injurious, an attack, or destructive. As a matter of fact, "the more that we believe conflict is solvable, the more likely we are to aim for a full resolution of our differences, a genuine transformation of the conflict, and the restoration of a positive relationship."[47] Conflict can be a pathway toward healing and restoration and be a vehicle for growth, development, and maturity. Many of the worship wars often left casualties. However, the positive outcome of them were the different historical worship awakenings that will be discussed further in other chapters.

Another obstacle that I was able to conclude from my interview with Bishop Waddell is the lack of adequate resources for the needed changes.[48] Resources are not just financial. If there is no growth numerically, then there is a lack of resources financially as well as the limited number of volunteers. In larger churches, resources and people are more accessible. However, in a ministry setting like Temple #203 with an average weekly attendance of around 75 - 100, some resources and investments are out of reach at this time.[49] That does not make the need go away; however, it just cannot be addressed or remedied. Worship is an area of investment that cannot be overlooked. There must be continued strategies, budgeting, and planning in order for it to evolve and become more culturally relevant.

There is a culture where the organizational structure of the church is set up where every major decision is governed by the executive board. In the local temple, the Senior Pastor is the head

---

[46] "Leadership Surveys Church Conflict" *Christianity Today* (2004).

[47] Bernard S. Mayer, *The Dynamics of Conflict: A Guide to Engagement and Intervention.* (San Francisco: Jossey-Bass, 2012.), Chp 4.

[48] Rex Waddell (Ministry Assessment), interviewed by Timothy Price, III, Fairview Heights, IL, May 23, 2018.

[49] Ibid., October 2018.

of that governing board.[50] Therefore, it is my assessment that it is easy for a congregation to become stagnant. John Maxwell famously stated, "Everything rises and falls on leadership."[51]

Sometimes sheep do not know that their needs are not getting met or that they can be better served. At the same time, they may know what they want but do not know how to access the solutions. Therefore, individuals become hostile without even knowing why. This is the power that the Senior Pastor has. He interprets according to scripture, education, prayer, and leading of the Holy Spirit concerning the needs of his flock.

When interpreting, it must be done effectively. Effective communication is very important. It helps to have clarity about different matters as well as helps articulate what is important. In ministry, effective communication is an educational experience that manifests God's grace in the lives of people. What we say as leaders and individuals in the church can either drive people to or away from us.

Therefore, it may be more effective, especially concerning the worship of the church, if the membership has ways to express their needs. There may be a large variation of desires; however, with effective communication and interpretation it can promote peace, healing, and restoration. It will give the members opportunity to voice how and what they feel may be beneficial for the journey in worship.

This ministry project is an outlet for them to be able to communicate those desires. Afterwards, the information can be communicated to the Senior Pastor and leaders who are responsible for serving in the different capacities for worship. After communication is done, it is essential to follow up by developing a system where

---

[50] "Church of The Living God C.W.F.F. National Brotherhood." Church of The Living God C.W.F.F. National Brotherhood. Accessed December 17, 2018 from http://www.ctlgcwff.org/

[51] John C. Maxwell Quotes. BrainyQuote.com, BrainyMedia Inc, 2019. Accessed May 27, 2019 from https://www.brainyquote.com/quotes/john_c_maxwell_600859

the needs of those and the one facilitating it are reciprocal to one another. In other words, it must be mutually reinforcing to create a fruitful worship experience.[52]

I was able to find seven health promoters for developing a system after everyone voices their needs. In Peter Steinke's book *Healthy Congregations*, he provided these: "purpose, appraisal and management of conflict, clarity, mood and tone, mature interaction, healing capacities, and a focus on resources."[53] These health promotors alter the focus and energy from the issues and weakness to the strength, options, and resources. The fruit of this accelerates the worship ministry of the church into a healthy direction, builds the morale, and growth will become a tangible asset once again at Temple #203. Temple #203 will be able to push past the obstacles and hindrances that have been discussed. They will also be able to move toward building a healthy worship ministry, church, community, and growth.

It must be clear that growth is not always numerical. Growth can be measured by how effective the church has become in the community of the ministry setting. A church does not have to be a megachurch in order to do mega ministry. Worship provides avenues for the congregation and community to display and celebrate their individual gifts in a corporate space to the glory of God. "Worship is the continuous outpouring of all that I am, all that I do, and all that I can ever become in light of a chosen or choosing God."[54]

Knowing the obstacles that hinder worship from being more substantive and effective for all generations will significantly promote opportunities for success in future planning for worship. Planning and implementation will become more innovative, strategic, honor integration, utilize various gifts, and unify the

---

[52] Peter L. Steinke *Healthy Congregations*. (Lanham, MD: Rowman & Littlefield Publishers, 2006), 27.

[53] Ibid., 4.

[54] Harold M. Best, *Unceasing Worship: Biblical Perspectives on Worship and the Arts*. (Downers Grove, IL: InterVarsity Press, 2003), 18.

church and community positively.[55] This next chapter is a broadened study of the community where Temple #203 is planted. This will help the leadership and volunteers who are a part of this ministry project see the variation of people who are part of the community. Knowing illuminates options for a variety of innovations musically and beyond because of who becomes the target audience and serving in the community.

---

[55] Matt Willmington, Silos in Ministry (Liberty University, 2016).

CHAPTER THREE

Theology of Community and Ministry

"The way we traditionally expressed Christianity may be in trouble, but the future may hold new expressions of the Christian faith every bit as effective, faithful, meaningful, and world-transforming as those we've know so far."[56] These words by Dan Kimball engage two things. One, the traditions of Christianity are in trouble because many of the traditions of Christianity have become ineffective in a world that is transforming. Second, what is ahead of us is going to revolutionize the Christian community. Many innovations and expressions have become increasingly visible in this age, especially in the area of worship. Worship is a vehicle and means of how we express our faith and love toward God that is evolving in the church.

The present-day influences such as the use of technology and music may be good, but the church must effectively create worship experiences that reach all ages and demographics in order to connect the body of Christ to the Lord and to each other. Therefore, this project proposes an ancient-future style of worship that does not totally reject any particular style or structure in worship. This particular style maintains a high view of Scripture, the doctrines of faith, and an emphasis on a transformative relationship between Jesus Christ and humanity.

---

[56] Dan Kimball, *Emerging Worship: Creating Worship Gatherings for New Generations* (Grand Rapids, MI: Zondervan, 2004.) ix.

Leaders in the church, especially those who serve in the area of worship, must become students of how worship is evolving and the changes happening in present culture. Therefore, assessing the current perspectives, innovations, and styles of worship in the church is worth discovery and assessment. This analysis will foster and promote positive results, helping the church to make the best use of new ideas from culture while maintaining a distinct identity of Christian worship.

Reggie McNeal's diagnosis of problems in the church echoes Dan Kimball's statement. McNeal declares, "the current church culture in North America is on life support."[57] After unmasking his feelings about Christianity in North America, he follows up by asking some tough questions and addressing some very important realities for the church in each chapter of his book. They are as follows:

1. The collapse of the church culture.
2. The shift from church growth to Kingdom growth.
3. A new reformation: Releasing God's people.
4. The return to Spiritual formation.
5. The shift from planning to preparation.
6. The rise of apostolic leadership.

However, the one that is most relevant to this topic and particular cause is "The Collapse of the Church Culture." McNeal concludes that the congregations in North America are existing off of people who are ages fifty-five and older.[58] When they die, so will the church. In this present culture, there is a shift taking place. The church has moved from ancient, medieval, to now modern. There is a denial in the church where the belief is that the culture will come back to its senses and the church will become prominent again. The collapse of the church is visible by the decrease of the succeeding generations that come to church.

---

[57] Reggie McNeal, *Present Future: Six Tough Questions for the Church* (Hoboken, NJ: John Wiley & Sons, 2003), 1.

[58] Ibid., 1.

Therefore, McNeal's conclusion about the church and his desire to see a new level of excitement in the church helped me realize there are some needed methodical changes in the church. Change does not mean erasing the principles or mission of the church. We must take on the challenge of learning the best practice for the evolving church through prayer, education, courage, and implementation.

In a climate where politics and economics continuously shift in the community, missional effectiveness and the lifestyle of worship must do the same. However, there are some who hold to the mindset that "If it isn't broke, don't fix it," while others are screaming that the traditional practices of the ancient and medieval church are not working for them. This inner conflict in the church makes the argument of McNeal relevant and justifiable. For instance, in the current ministry setting for this project, the worship of the church has reached its traditional peak and become stagnate. When there is stagnation, "little or no statistical growth (numerical, spiritual, or otherwise) and minimal impact on the surrounding culture," is visible, revealing the serious needs that must be addressed.[59]

The intent of this project is not to cancel out all of this ministry setting's traditional position of worship. It is to illumine to the church and leadership that they will benefit from embracing and practicing worship from a new and different approach. This approach includes an ancient – future style of worship. This style will be effective because it embraces diverse styles of music and innovations in worship.

There are generations seeking refuge, salvation, and worship experiences that mirror their culture, customs, and ways of life. In this particular ministry setting, the church has not presented a format and position that currently meets the needs of multiple generations. The challenge of holding onto yesterday while embracing the future has not been mastered. The music, rituals, and sacred practices in worship will either reveal a connect or disconnect with the coming generations. Therefore, flexibility, fluidity, with balance is crucial when change is being considered.

---

[59] Warren Bird, Ed Stetzer, and Elmer Towns, *11 Innovations in the Local Church*. (Ventura, CA: Regal Books, 2007), 14.

In communities all over the world there are numerous Christian denominations with various worship practices. Some feature more traditional music while others use a more contemporary style. Some denominations that I am familiar with are Baptist, Church of God in Christ, African Methodist Episcopal, and Non-Denominational Churches. I have had the pleasure of serving in various roles of the Music and Worship Ministry of churches under these denominations.

Each one of these denominations are a part of my faith journey and have influenced how I worship. Denominations play a central role in American life.[60] An individual's religious affiliation identifies worship preference, ethnicity, doctrinal belief, political stance, and even social status. Denomination is one of the most common ways in society that identifies one's cultural tradition and social belonging. Whichever denominational preference one has, there must be innovative expressions to reach diverse groups of people.

Theology of Community

There are three major divisions of Christianity. Those divisions are Roman Catholic, Protestant, and Orthodox. The denominations that I mentioned above are all Protestant and have been a part of my faith and ecclesiological tradition. The root word for Protestant is "protest." In spite of the original protest against some of the practices of the Catholic church, the focuses of any Protestant church should be positive rather than negative. The true meaning of their protest is to make certain affirmations, to give testimony on behalf of certain things.[61]

Protestants affirm their faith through public testimony and declaration. They have strong convictions about the Bible, salvation, the ministry of all believers. My ministry project focuses on worship in Protestant churches. I will provide insight from those churches I

---

[60] Ibid., 54.

[61] Richard Allen, *The Doctrine and Discipline of the African Methodist Episcopal Church* (Chapel Hill, NC: University of North Carolina at Chapel Hill, 2016), 16.

researched and experienced. I will discuss their individual worship features which include music, preaching, and the use of sacrament.

AFRICAN METHODIST EPISCOPAL DENOMINATIONAL WORSHIP

In 1816, the African Methodist Episcopal church was founded by Rev. Richard Allen of Philadelphia, PA. One of the most thorough resources about the AME Church was published in 1817, "The Doctrines and Discipline of the African Methodist Episcopal Church," by Richard Allen and Jacob Tapisco. There have been 50 editions of this document. The latest that I was able to find was published in 2016. This document is meant to be a companion to the Bible, not a replacement. It provides history on the organization, its teachings, beliefs, and the practices of the early AME Church.

This Protestant denomination was inaugurated by a black Methodist who wanted to be independent from white Methodists. This global Christian body is presently on five continents and in over three dozen countries.[62] I had the opportunity of serving at one of the historical mother churches of this denomination. The AME church is known for focusing on the civil rights of African Americans. The worship of the AME church is a liturgical and charismatic blend. Liturgy is discipline and focused work created by the people. To be charismatic means to be spirit-filled with personality. Some of those traditional areas where this blend is visible and also became critical areas of influence for this project are:

Music

In 1840, the best vocalists who were members of Bethel Church in Philadelphia got together and organized a choir with the permission of the Bishop. This was a radical move because the "old people" were opposed to singing by notes. The tradition of the church was

---

[62] Ibid., 15.

to appoint someone to lead the congregation in singing.[63] One person sung while the congregation listened. Over time, choirs, also formerly known as a "vocal soiree" became acceptable and an important component in worship. The effect of music in the sanctuary was considered as thrilling as some of the most spiritual sermons preached and also paved the way for the use of the organ and other instruments as time progressed.[64]

Preaching

Preaching under the AME church had an exterior of education and knowledge with an evangelical witness.[65] The strength of the preaching position of the AME preacher is that it made the knowledge and salvation of Jesus intimately connected so that the hearer could experience Jesus on the inside.

Sacraments

The sacraments used in worship are more than badges or tokens of Christianity, they are signs of grace and God's will toward humanity.[66] They are practiced in worship to strengthen and confirm faith in God. The two sacraments that are counted as important displays in worship are Baptism, which is a sign of profession and regeneration. The Lord's Supper is the other. It is a sign of love and a sacrament of redemption by Christ's death.[67]

---

[63] Daniel Alexander Payne, *History of the African Methodist Episcopal Church* (North Stratford, NH: Ayer, 2000), 452.

[64] Ibid., 453 - 454.

[65] A. Owens, *Formation of the African Methodist Episcopal Church in the Nineteenth Century: Rhetoric of Identification* (London: Palgrave Macmillan, 2016).

[66] Richard Allen, *The Doctrines and Discipline of the African Methodist Episcopal Church* (Chapel Hill, NC: University of North Carolina at Chapel Hill Library, 2016), 19.

[67] Ibid., 21.

The three critical areas that were analyzed in this denomination are important areas to highlight because they are areas of important religious expression. The use of liturgy in the church appealed to the upper class and educated. It brought respect in worship. However, the charismatic approach made worship and the connection with God more intimate and personal.

BAPTIST DENOMINATIONAL WORSHIP

The Baptist denomination originated out of England in the seventeenth century. The belief of the Baptists is that God continues to speak to His people. God "hath yet more light to break forth from his word."[68] Baptist theology rests upon their fundamental beliefs concerning the authority of Scripture, religious liberty, sacrament, and the believer's baptism.

In McBeth's exhaustive research on the Baptist church, I was able to conclude that the greatest differences and areas of tension in the Baptist Church had to do with race and how worship was going to be expressed in each church. However, there was no tension concerning the use of liturgical practices in worship in the denomination as a whole. Liturgy is an important part of the worship culture in the Baptist Denomination. It provides parameters for religious practice that help develop, energize, and shape the faith of each Christian believer that has gathered in the community of faith.[69]

The practice of liturgy gave strength to how believers served God. It is central to this denomination. However, it varied in each congregation. As stated before, liturgy is the work of the people. Therefore, history has shown that churchmen formed their own independent congregations so that they could institute their

---

[68] H. Leon. McBeth, *Baptist Heritage: Four Centuries of Baptist Witness* (Nashville, TN: Broadman and Holman, 2016), 1.

[69] Rodney Kennedy, and Derek Christopher Hatch, *Gathering Together: Baptists at Work in Worship* (Eugene, OR: Pickwick Publications, 2013), ix.

own biblical practices. The areas in worship where tension and disagreement are most visible are found in the following sections:

Music

Many of the different groups under the Baptist Denomination have printed through their own publishing house books used for worship called Hymnals. Hymnals are selected songs that can be performed by a solo, ensemble, choir, and with or without instrumentation. For example, The New National Baptist Hymnal was published in 1990, The Primitive Baptist Hymnal was first published in 1841, and The Baptist Hymnal was first released in 1956 and its latest version in 2008.

There are many more published that include songs that appeal to certain regions, races and cultures, functions, and occasions. However, they do not appeal to the younger generations. This area of weakness makes worship more exclusive to certain demographics and ages, rather than inclusive for all generations. Hymns help shape theology, worship, and establishes reverence and piety in the denomination. They promote congregational singing and corporate involvement which is a key element of Baptist worship in the twenty-first century.[70]

Preaching

The music and preaching are two separate entities in worship. In the Baptist church, expository sermons are delivered week after week in worship with the intent to "win from people a response to the gospel, a response from attitude, impulse, and thought."[71] The Gospel is a very important part of the preaching message in the Baptist church.

---

[70] David W. Music and Paul Akers Richardson, *"I Will Sing the Wondrous Story"*: *A History of Baptist Hymnody in North America* (Macon Ga.: Mercer University Press, 2011), Preface.

[71] Dennis Price, "Measurement of the Effect of Preaching and Preaching Plus Small Group Dialogue in One Baptist Church" *Journal for the Scientific Study of Religion* 19 (June, 1980): 186.

In my personal experience, I concluded that an individual who is proclaiming the Word of God has not successfully done so in the Baptist church if they have not included in their message about the death, burial, and resurrection of Jesus Christ.

Sacraments

Similar to the AME Church, the two sacraments that are important practices in worship of the Baptist church is baptism and the Lord's Supper. They are considered areas of obedience to their faith. The Lord's Supper was observed weekly by some of the more ancient and traditional Baptists, but less often by most.[72]

Throughout history, many different interpretations of scripture and how worship should be practiced caused division. Areas of debate included baptism, infant baptism, total immersion or sprinkling, atonement, laying on of hands, singing as a part of public worship, open or closed communion, etc.[73] Because of that, different groups were established out of the Baptist church. Some include National Baptists, General Baptists, Southern Baptists, Primitive Baptists, Missionary Baptists, and numerous others. The Baptist denomination is a very viable entity of the Christian faith.

CHURCH OF GOD IN CHRIST DENOMINATIONAL WORSHIP

The Church of God in Christ also known as COGIC is a Pentecostal Denomination established in 1907 by Charles Harrison Mason in Memphis, TN who actually left a Baptist Church in Lexington, Mississippi.[74] Mason's visit to the famous Azusa Street Revival shifted

---

[72] H. Leon. McBeth, *Baptist Heritage: Four Centuries of Baptist Witness*. (Nashville, TN.: Broadman and Holman, 2016), 97.

[73] Ibid., 65.

[74] Eileen Southern, *The Music of Black Americans: A History* (New York: W. W. Norton & Company, 2006), 262.

his doctrinal beliefs. He received the baptism of the Holy Ghost with the evidence of speaking in other tongues. From his Pentecostal experience, he reorganized the Church of God in Christ as a Holiness church. The worship expression of this denomination centers around the necessity of the Holy Spirt and spiritual expression in every aspect of worship. I will assess the same critical areas.

Music

Music is a very important aspect to worship. The goal of the music ministry is to create an atmosphere for the Spirit of God to have free course. The COGIC has its own hymnal that governs the sound of the church. The music of the church embraces instruments that include piano, organ, guitar, and drums. Choirs are common in the worship of the church. The traditional church had "Praise Services" that included call and response congregational songs. This is still a continued practice in most local churches.

Preaching

In the COGIC, no member is authorized to preach representing the COGIC without a license or ordination.[75] The preaching done in COGIC is often an expository sermon that is lively, rhythmic, and spirited. It is usually accompanied with music in and out of the sermon that is culturally interpreted as the musician "backing up the preacher."

Sacraments

COGIC calls the practices of the sacrament the ordinances of the church. The word ordinance represents the Old Testament that refers to matters of ritual.[76] There are three that the Church recognizes to be practiced in worship. They are The Lord's Supper, Feet Washing,

---

[75] *Official Manual with the Doctrines and Discipline of the Church of God in Christ, 1973.* (Memphis, TN: Church of God in Christ, Pub. Board, 1991), 133.

[76] Ibid., 75.

and Water Baptism. These ordinances are signs of the grace of God in Christ, and the benefits of the covenant of God's grace for believers. They are practiced in worship to express believers' faith and allegiance to God.[77] The presence of the Holy Spirit is very vital in the life and worship of this denomination. It is a necessity for the believer and in worship service. It inspires atmosphere and discipleship.[78]

NON-DENOMINATIONAL WORSHIP

A Non-Denominational church is a community of believers who have chosen to separate themselves from being affiliated with any of the historic denominations of Christianity. Any church that is non-denominational functions without any official doctrine or customs. Non-denominational churches are typically founded by an individual pastor. Their biggest appeal to Christians is the fact that they are non-traditional.

In most non-denominational churches, the worship style is more flexible, fluid, and in most situations contemporary. Most non-denominational churches vary in theology and style of worship. Just like the other denominations, these critical areas that are practiced in worship had to be assess. They influenced this project.

Music

Preaching is not limited to the spoken word.[79] Worship music in many non-denominational churches include exhortation and preaching of the Word of God through music. One of the positives of this particular music ministry setting is they have not gotten rid of the traditions of old which include hymns. Praise and celebration should always include hymns in my personal assessment. In many

---

[77] Ibid., 76.

[78] Ibid., 45-46.

[79] Ibid., 187.

non-denominational churches, hymns have become endangered species battling against praise choruses and video projectors.[80] Hymns connect the struggles of the past while the contemporary music connect us with the experiences of today. There should be a balance with the two.

Preaching

In this particular church, the pastor preaches an expository message that includes a mixture of scripture and real-life scenarios. In this particular denomination, the preachers communicate in ways that they are comfortable. It is fluid according to culture. This is important because the more aware we are of our value, identity, gifts, and abilities the greater passion and conviction we possess when communicating.[81]

Sacraments

The three sacraments that area observed in this denomination are the same used in COGIC. They are Baptism, the Lord's Supper, and Feet Washing. They are used as a sign of the New Covenant ordained of Christ. After careful observation, research and assessment, I concluded that the ministry setting where my ministry project will be conducted is in a non-denominational Church. This particular ministry setting under this fellowship has a more traditional style of worship. However, most non-denominational churches are open and receptive to the different cultures, styles, and social issues because they have no formal allegiance to any religious structure.[82] Therefore,

---

[80] Robert J. Morgan, *Then Sings My Soul Book 2:150 of the World's Greatest Hymn Stories* (Nashville, TN: Thomas Nelson Publishers, 2003), xi.

[81] "Self Discovery." Reading. 2016. Accessed March 23, 2018. (myclasses. southernuniversity.edu), 2.

[82] Kate Shellnutt, "Protestants Keep Ditching Denominations." *Christianity Today/News and Reporting* (2017). Accessed April, 7, 2019 from https://www. christianitytoday.com/news/2017/july/rise-of-nons-protestants-denominations-nondenominational.html

I concluded that there would be less difficulty trying to promote change. The former denominations all have strong areas of liturgy and tradition that will be difficult to challenge or change for the time and purpose of this project.

Biblical Foundation

The previous section presented concise information on the various denominations that I have served and researched. The doctrines of these denominations influence how members of a fellowship practice worship based off theological interpretation. Therefore, attempting to make changes in worship of a church where the works and beliefs of the people govern how worship should be carried out makes that goal of change increasingly difficult. Yet, I believe the use of biblical instruction will have a greater influence on what may seem difficult, granting greater possibilities in the end.

The three areas that I assessed in each denomination were music, preaching, and the sacrament. Each of these entities are ways that God communicates His heart as well as how we connect with Him in worship. In scripture, God used narratives, poetry, imagery, songs, and other ways to express Himself.[83] His message was clear and concise. The goal for this project and beyond is to do the same. Every aspect of worship must be practiced, planned, and prepared clearly and concisely so that it would be embraced and effective to those intended to reach.

The Bible is filled with theological concepts of worship that support what worship really is and is about. The New Testament does not really talk about music in worship as much as the Old Testament does. The Old Testament illumines the importance of music in worship. Some songwriters in the Old Testament were Moses, Hannah, David, and Solomon. Their songs were filled with

---

[83] Week 1: *"God's Communication Methodology"* (online assignment introduction, MIN7062 Communication Skills for Ministry, South University). Accessed April 8, 2018.

their own personal experiences with God. They also centered on the mighty acts and nature of God.

Individual churches and denominations have more leeway when choosing what worship practices and style of music will best suit their church. This is where liturgy is established. However, secular influences in worship have increased in how churches are deciding to practice worship. There are positives and negatives to that reality. However, I conclude that the sound of worship in the church should never be confused between what is sacred and secular.

God wants to be glorified through praise, worship, doctrine, cultural influences, and the Bible. According to 2 Timothy 3:16-17, all scripture is written for instruction and encouragement to walk in obedience to His will. Below are core passages that are relevant, specific, and critical to the goal of this project. They all have been matched with some principles of worship that will further strengthen the purpose of the ministry project as well as its contribution to the ministry setting.

WORSHIP MUST BE A DECISION:

"O Lord, You are my God; I will exalt You, I will give thanks to Your name; for You have worked wonders, plans formed long ago, with perfect faithfulness," (Isa 25:1). The prophet Isaiah spoke about his uneasiness concerning the judgements of God that not only threatened a single nation, but almost the whole world.[84] He exhorted that there needed to be a decision made by humankind. In his concern and grief, because of the sinful state of humankind, he took courage to preach a message that encouraged those to fear God. Choosing to trust and worship God has greater advantage of receiving His grace rather than the possible calamities they were facing.

---

[84] Jean Calvin and William Pringle, *Commentary on the Book of the Prophet Isaiah* Vol.2 (Grand Rapids, MI: Baker Book House, 1979), 189.

Isaiah did not hesitate to display his confidence in the omniscience and truth of the Lord.[85] He remembered that God is reliable and consistent in every way. Therefore, we must be led, influenced, and encouraged to make the decision to delight and praise His name.[86] Worship is more than a feeling. It is a decision that is manifested from belief in God's sayings and revelation of His Word. Therefore, worship must reveal His truth so that it will not only be an emotional response but also a matter of intent. When we sing about the deeds of God, it should encourage excitement and thanksgiving in the worship experience.

WORSHIP MUST BE DONE IN SPIRIT AND TRUTH:

"God is spirit, and those who worship Him must worship in spirit and truth," (John 4:24). This passage is commonly used in discussions about worship. However, it should be considered more than just a common expression; it is the law of life for all worshippers.[87] It is more than how we worship, but an argument of where we should worship. Christians who seek to be ambassadors for Christ must always be wary of falling into the trap of arguing about the "right" place of worship or the "right" denomination.[88] Jesus did not technically argue with the Samaritan woman during their discussion.

This discussion was an attempt to have a theological argument. However, Jesus turned her question around so that she could confront

---

[85] Carl Wilhelm Eduard Nägelsbach, Samuel T. Lowrie, and Dunlop Moore, *The Prophet Isaiah: Theologically and Homiletically Expounded*. (Eugene, OR: Wipf & Stock Publishers, 2007), 277.

[86] Jean Calvin and William Pringle, *Commentary on the Book of the Prophet Isaiah*. Vol. 2 (Grand Rapids, MI: Baker Book House, 1979), 190.

[87] John Peter Lange, *The Gospel According to John* (Grand Rapids, MI: Zondervan, 1960), John 4:24

[88] David S. Dockery, *The New American Commentary* Vol. 25 (Nashville, TN: Broadman & Holman, 1991), John 4:21-24.

herself.[89] When one worships God in *spirit and truth,* they lay aside the entanglements of ancient ceremonies. The intent of worship is to make people confront themselves. Worship must always be a spiritual encounter that is done in spirit and truth. Our motives of worship must be done in spirit and truthfulness. The more we encounter God, the more He reveals Himself to us. Any practice of worship that does not include those two important elements is considered a form and mode of religion that should never be a substitute for the seeking of our hearts to worship Him and fulfill His Will.

WORSHIP MUST EMBODY OUR TESTIMONY:

"Come and see the works of God, who is awesome in His deeds toward the sons of men. He turned the sea into dry land; they passed through the river on foot; there let us rejoice in Him," (Ps 66:5-6). God delivered Israel from the trials that they endured. In this passage of scripture, an indirect censure is passed upon that almost led men to neglect the praises of God where they blindly overlooked the operations of God's hand.[90] Worship must bring us to a place where our thoughts are directed on God. Humankind does not have to look further than themselves to discover the greatness of God.

This passage of scripture is an illustration of many that reminds us from the testimony of the psalmist that he called upon God, God heard him, therefore he rendered thanksgiving unto God[91] Worship is born out of the things that God has done. When presenting music in worship, it must reflect that reality. It must confirm the evidence of what God has done and can do for humankind.

---

[89] Ibid., John 4:24.

[90] Jean Calvin and William Pringle, *Commentary on the Book of Psalms* Vol. 2 (Grand Rapids, MI: Baker Book House, 1979), 468.

[91] Carl Bernhard Moll, *The Psalms* (Grand Rapids, MI: Zondervan, 1960), Psalm 66:5-6.

GOD RESPONDS TO OUR WORSHIP:

"Yet You are holy, O You who are enthroned upon the praises of Israel," (Ps 22:3). Humankind complains about God withdrawing from them especially in times of tribulation. Then we find ourselves overwhelmed with grief, discouragement, and fear. Some think that the eternal and immutable state of God makes Him detached to the afflictions that David experienced.[92] However, this passage does not refer to who He is in heaven, but what He has revealed to David and does toward men. David altered his attention on the evidence of God's grace. He referenced Him as holy because it is against God's nature to leave humankind in a miserable state of despair and solace.

Because He is such a liberal God towards His people, He has chosen to continue to bestow blessings upon His chosen people. Therefore, we have no reason to be mute. Wherever we find ourselves, our worship provides a dwelling place for the presence of God. The songs of praise that we lift in the sanctuary forms a throne for God and ascends unto Him as cloud of incense summonsing His presence.[93] Worship is not limited or confined to the sanctuary only; worship relieves stress and concern of where is God for the believer and unbeliever. He is able to be found in worship.

Each one of these principles and the scriptures attached with them help conclude more clearly that worship is more than denominational rituals and practices that are reflections of our heritage. What we do in worship must embody these principles and approaches found in the scripture. I do not believe that the traditions of humanity are necessarily practices that God frowns upon. However, I do believe that the rituals and traditions that we display in worship are no longer enough for the generations ahead.

God created a purpose for all creation. He intentionally, fearfully and wonderfully made all creation so that humanity would mirror and reflect the image of Himself. From the beginning of creation,

---

[92] Jean Calvin and William Pringle, *Commentary on the Book of Psalms* Vol. 2 (Grand Rapids, MI: Baker Book House, 1979), 363.

[93] Ibid,, Psalm 22:3.

God calculated in all wisdom how humankind was to look and act. In Psalm 19, scripture reveals that all creation is created to praise God. However, humankind has been separated from all other created things to produce fear of and reverence to God.

The wisdom of God supersedes all manners of human understanding. Worship is a lifestyle. It is more than coming together on Sundays in our various denominations. It is a part of our created nature that cannot be hidden. Harold Best stated, "We begin with one fundamental fact about worship: at this very moment, and for as long as this world endures, everybody inhabiting it is bowing down and serving something or someone – an artifact, a person, an institution, an idea, a spirit or God through Christ."[94] God desires above all things that the posture of our worship is biblically sound, philosophically understood, and done out of obedience.

That obedience reflects the fear of the Lord and influences our conduct and possesses the heart while we walk in wisdom of the Word of God. Worship should make one choose a path of righteousness rather than indulgence of worldly lusts. The influences of music, preaching, sacrament, and any other expressions done in worship should always influence a response toward and from God. Some of those responses include salvation, peace, hope, grace, healing, etc. In worship we are nurtured, God is glorified, and this worship project will courageously push the ministry setting to "transcend the pressures of culture, peer acceptance, and ecclesiastical nuances…"[95]

THEOLOGY OF MINISTRY

After substantive research, I have concluded that culture has greatly influenced the way churches practice worship. Megachurches, huge edifices, and culturally inspired worship services have been created

---

[94] Harold M. Best, *Unceasing Worship: Biblical Perspectives on Worship and the Arts* (Downers Grove, IL: InterVarsity Press, 2003), 17.

[95] Vernon M. Whaley, *The Dynamics of Corporate Worship* (Virginia Beach, VA: Academx Publishing Services, 2009), 32.

to reach multi-generations, ethnicities, and the unchurched. Many of the modern churches have structured facilities that no longer look like traditional church sanctuaries. The worship services have evolved from being solemn, ceremonially focused, condemning or judgmental to services that focus on self-esteem, empathy, and language that communicates hope while building a relationship with God.

Modern churches have implemented contemporary worship styles, family-oriented sermons, day cares, athletic facilities, etc. These changes represent how the church is responding to cultural influences rather than influencing the larger culture. Richard Niebuhr argues that culture has gained greater influence in the American church and in every aspect of religious life.[96] The church has become more occupied with being relevant to culture rather than revealing more of Christ.

Historically there has been an enduring problem between "Christianity and civilization."[97] Christians have been seeking ways to be culturally relevant in the church. This pursuit is a necessity; however, it must never compromise biblical integrity and our faith in Jesus Christ. Jesus must never be limited or defined by the conditions of culture. I agree with his position. Many cultural antagonists in different times would argue against Niebuhr's conclusion. They would argue that this position induces men to rely more on the grace of God instead of human achievement.[98] This is one of the major issues that underlines many of the worship wars, conflicts in the church, and the disagreement between generations in the church. The answers to the problems of human culture is one thing, Christian answers are another that are accomplished through the works of humanity.[99]

Culture is the social life of all humanity. Humanity has created

---

[96] H. Richard Niebuhr, *Christ & Culture* (New York: HarperCollins World, 2003), 179.

[97] Ibid., 1.

[98] Ibid., 6.

[99] Ibid., 2.

language, habits, ideas, beliefs, customs, social organizations, inherited artifacts, technical processes, and values.[100] A combination of the created things of humankind with the non-cultural norms created by God can be difficult. It is a perfect God mingling with an imperfect people to bring about perfected end. The possibility of this is challenging. One of these will begin to be revealed more. According to Niebuhr, humanity has been revealed more than the Christ we are to be promoting in Christianity.

In the modern church, Jesus must be adequately defined through scripture. Niebuhr argues that there must be balance between Christ and culture. In the upcoming chapters, I will provide a basic roadmap that includes scripture and innovations that were assessed through cultural research. However, the information provided will underline that our significance and loyalty to Jesus Christ in worship does not mean isolation or total separation from culture.

The power and authority of the Holy Spirit and the name of Jesus cannot be isolated from culture or humanity. Christ came to give hope, aspiration, and perfection to our faith.[101] Therefore, we must look deeper to Christ to find answers to what we are looking for and need in worship. Historically, people were attracted to Christ because of how the Christian message was harmonized with culture in worship gatherings.

God is a real savior who desires to positively impact our real issues. Therefore, He does not need to be conformed to our cultural expectations. The vehicles of culture must be agents that connect all humanity to Him. What man has created cannot be separated from the sovereignty of God. Niebuhr noted, "They cannot separate the works of human culture from the grace of God, for all those works are possible only by grace. Neither can they separate the experience of grace from cultural activity; for how can men love the unseen God in response to His love without serving the visible brother in human society."[102]

---

[100] Ibid., 32.

[101] Ibid., 83.

[102] Ibid., 119.

The balance between who we are culturally and whose we are being implemented in our Christianity is not an impossible task. It must be executed with an awareness of the conditions of culture. We must have a measured opinion of how we will be involved in culture and our faithfulness serving the Lord. We must never act alone when making decisions for a higher purpose. We must always allow the grace of God to guide and work through us regardless of any areas of ignorance or limitations we have.

A field of study that exists and assists churches in adapting and developing creative expressions in worship is Ethnodoxology, which is a theological and practical study of how and why people of diverse cultures praise and glorify the true and living God as revealed in the Bible.[103] Every expression of music in worship does not speak to every culture and generation. Therefore, this study is beneficial to helping churches understand, embrace, and show how culture needs to be expressed in a way where Jesus Christ is magnified.

Christianity is universal. Jesus came to save all nations. Scripture says, "When they saw Him, they worshiped Him; but some were doubtful...Go therefore and make disciples of all nations, baptizing them in the name of the Father and the Son and the Holy Spirit." (Matt 28:17,19). This further clarifies that worship has become a tool of evangelism. David Wheeler and Vernon Whaley stated that "If the worship we do and the evangelism we give ourselves to is biblical, it should sculpt, form, and shape us."[104] This is why worship must be seen through a widened lens in order for it to become more effective. It is a tool of evangelism where people have the ability to be drawn closer to God. As disciples we spread our faith and point nonbelievers to the light.

Therefore, the shared experience of worship in a corporate ministry setting should be dynamic and intentional. There must be

---

[103] Ian Collinge, *A Kaleidoscope of Doxology: Exploring Ethnodoxology and Theology* 2010 (DVD Resource).

[104] David Wheeler, and Vernon Whaley, *The Great Commission to Worship: Biblical Principles for Worship-Based Evangelism* (Nashville, TN: B & H Publishing, 2011), 49.

an expectation of results when planning and preparing worship. It takes on several attributes. Worship becomes formational.[105] It is a two-way street. We worship, yet our relationship with God is being enriched. Out of our worship, there is development, structure, and things take shape while in worship. Our lives are aligned and develop in a way that reflect God's glory.

1. **God changes our language.** He not only speaks to us, but he speaks through us. "Then the Lord stretched out His hand and touched my mouth, and the Lord said to me, Behold, I have put My words in your mouth" (Jer 1:9).

2. **God shapes our lives.** Our desire increases to live passionately for Him. We radiate His love and are passionate about showing that same love to the world. "And hope does not disappoint, because the love of God has been poured out within our hearts through the Holy Spirit who has given to us" (Rom 5:5).

3. **God gives us the desire to be obedient**. "Let us not lose heart in doing good, for in due time we will reap if we do not grow weary" (Gal 6:9). His will becomes our will and God blesses that obedience.

4. **God blesses our hands.** Worship gives us the ability to become successful by forming and arranging our lives so that His glory becomes reflective in each aspect of our life. "The Lord will open for you His good storehouse, the heavens, to give rain to your land in its season and to bless all the work of your hand" (Deut 28:12).

Worship then becomes transformational. The transformational element of worship exposes mankind to who God is while in the act of worship. We are changed from old to new. Scripture says, "And do not be conformed to this world, but be transformed by the renewing of your mind, so that you may prove what the will of God is, that

---

[105] David Wheeler and Vernon M. Whaley, *Worship and Witness: Becoming a Great Commission Worshiper* (Nashville, TN: LifeWay Press, 2012), 8.

which is good and acceptable and perfect," (Rom 12:2). Worship renews, restores, and changes us. The more we spend time with Him, the more we will be transformed in the process.

God takes the broken places and changes us in the process. The word *change* in the Greek means "to cause one thing to cease and another to take its place."[106] Worship is a journey where God reveals Himself, we are convicted by the Spirit, we profess our faith, are forgiven, and are changed while spending time with Him in worship.

Worship is also relational. It is a vertical relationship that affects our horizontal relationships. How we relate to God affects how we relate with each other. "Countless prodigal sons and daughters today have run from God yet are still desperate for a renewed relationship with the Father."[107] Relational worship is His heart responding and connecting to the hearts of humanity. It is love responding to love. God is a person, and in the depth of His mighty nature, He thinks, wills, enjoys, feels, loves, desires and suffers as any other person may.[108] When time is spent in worship, it heightens humankind's desire for, dependence on, and delight in Him. It is an established connection between created and creator that is upward and horizontal.

1. Upward:
   a. God is delighted when the needs of all creation have been fulfilled by Him.
   b. God nurtures His relationship with man by revealing Himself more deeply.
   c. God opens the door for humanity to have a personal and genuine relationship with Him.
2. Horizontal:
   a. The attitudes and spirits with earthly relationships how one treats another is nurtured.
   b. Relating to believers and unbelievers is affected.

---

[106] Ibid., 82.

[107] Ibid., 70.

[108] Ibid., 50.

    c.   It is an evangelistic experience that creates fruitful and nurturing relationships which includes relationships with those in leadership and in business.

Worship is Missional. "The word missional has emphasis upon missions but should not be considered an extraneous task or an activity. It is an activity that believers take on as followers of Christ."[109] "Being missional is living daily an authentic and intentional life of worship that embodies the ministry passion of Christ."[110] It is a passionate lifestyle that is visible in and out of the confines of any church structure. We carry the Word of God to the world and make disciples of men by bringing them closer to God. Worship is an evangelistic tool where out of our obedience and desire we become the hands and feet of God. There is an exposed passion for all humanity. It becomes increasingly difficult to resist from loving on others. It becomes a daily motivation reflecting the relationship God has with humankind.

Worship reproduces witnesses as individuals represent Jesus through their behaviors. Reproducible worship has influence and the power to make an eternal difference in the lives of all humanity. When worship becomes intentional, it is a progression and journey that includes faith and experience. These different dimensions of worship cause one to reflect over a theology of worship. It is more than entertainment and music.

THEOLOGICAL AWARENESS FOR MINISTRY

The fluidity of each section up to this point helps cultivate a greater theological awareness for worship. That awareness means to have an understanding about the major theological issues in the current worship of the church. In the ministry setting for this project, I was

---

[109] Ibid., 103.

[110] Ibid., 124.

able to identify that some of those issues include the lack of personnel in the music ministry, balance of styles of music in worship, and set goals.

The church needs to grow the music staff, whether they are volunteer or paid. In the long run, integrity, consistency, competence, responsibility, dependability, and productivity always pay off when there is a unified team serving toward a common goal in worship.[111] The day of the "one man show" is over. God uses people. Music is not the only component in worship. However, worship cannot be minimalized. Next to theology, the first and highest honor in worship is music.[112] Therefore, it is essential that one of the greatest investments in the church should be in the ministry of music.

This ministry setting must not totally reject any particular style or structure of worship. The church shows that it has a high regard and view of scripture as seen in the doctrines of their faith. However, it must be further embraced and emphasized that our relationships are ever evolving and transforming with Jesus Christ.[113] The church can be traditional, contemporary, ancient, future, and biblical all at the same time. This causes worship to be seeker-sensitive on the emerging generations of unchurched people as well as the churchgoers. It is also important to note that all present traditions were once innovations that someone introduced as a new way of doing things.[114]

The goals of worship must be inviting for all people. We all have needs and we all need each other.[115] Having an awareness helps the

---

[111] John C. Maxwell, *The 360 Leader: Developing Your Influence from Anywhere in the Organization* (Nashville, TN: Thomas Nelson, 2011), 145, 183.

[112] Elmer T. Towns and Vernon M. Whaley, *Worship Through the Ages* (Nashville, TN: Broadman & Holman, 2012), 108.

[113] Warren Bird, Ed Stetzer, and Elmer Towns, *11 Innovations in the Local Church* (Ventura, CA: Regal Books, 2007), 99.

[114] Ibid., 236.

[115] Ibid., 63.

congregation focus on the larger Kingdom mission that is diverse, creative, and innovative where worship becomes more inclusive and fulfills the goals it is set to fulfill. There must be solid biblical principles harmonized with intentional consideration of the people who will be served in worship.

"An effective method is always the application of a principle to culture, so we must look behind every method to see if it is based on biblical principle."[116] The collaboration between worship and cultural influences can be innovative. However, if that collaboration causes the practices of worship to be lost in the midst of cultural innovations; then worship becomes ineffective, entertaining only, and self-serving. Individuals turn into consumers rather than disciples of faith. Then church will eventually be in trouble.

Changes in Culture

Change is constant. Therefore, the circumstances and needs of each generation must be carefully assessed. Cultures change, people change, desires change, and worship methods change. Those changes are influencing the church to be different in worship expression, expressions which include cutting-edge methods of doing church. What is done today may not be good for tomorrow. As stated before, fluidity with balance is necessary in the life of worship in the church.

Cultures and climates are changing; however, the missional effectiveness of the church is not. A few critical areas in ministry that I would like to reiterate and briefly highlight for the first time of some that have influenced the culture of worship in the church as well as this project are *approach to preaching, technology and media, music, technology and media, and music*. Without any change in these areas, generations are subject to being left out and segregated. Change promotes inclusion in worship for multiple generations and cultures.

---

[116] Ibid., 241.

Approach to Preaching

A form of preaching takes place during the music in worship when worship leaders testify, proclaim God's power, and sing songs that contain solid theological messages. The Word of God is proclaimed, and individuals are pointed toward God. "It is our privilege to help people see how the Gospel functions in every part of their lives."[117] Those who are worship leaders who happen to be songwriters are literally preaching to music. The realities of the Bible are brought to life through singing and musical presentations. "When preaching is an act of worship, the listener's heart is stirred by the vision of God and the Spirit of God says far more to him than what the minister declares from the pulpit."[118]

Technology and Media

Technology and media are other areas that must be analyzed. No matter what style of worship is in the life of a church, technology has to become a major part of worship in this age. "Anthropologists have noted that culture consists of all learned beliefs and behaviors."[119] Technology influences culture and provides human beings ways to communicate in a way that has evolved with culture.

In worship, technology plays a large role. The usage of large screens for video feed, PowerPoint presentations, high-tech lighting, smoke machines, digital creativity, and other things attract emerging worshippers of this age. "Many churches have realized that the internet need not be a tool of isolation but can be a tool for connection."[120]

---

[117] Bob Kauflin, *Worship Matters: Leading Others to Encounter with Greatness of God*. (Wheaton, IL: Crossway Books, 2008), 130.

[118] Vernon M Whaley, *Called to Worship: From the Dawn of Creation to the Final Amen* (Nashville, TN: Thomas Nelson, 2009), 281-282.

[119] R.H. Robbins, *Global Problems and the Culture of Capitalism* (Boston, MA: Pearson, 2008), 4.

[120] Warren Bird, Ed Stetzer, and Elmer Towns, *11 Innovations in the Local Church*. (Ventura, CA: Regal Books, 2007), 161.

Technology is a great tool in churches to help further share the Gospel when used appropriately and effectively.

Music

Music is a major component in worship that is ever-changing. It is also the center focus for this ministry project. Churches are changing to more charismatic and contemporary styles of worship and liturgy. The Latin meaning of contemporary is "with or at the time." This contemporary style is currently known as Praise and Worship. It is musically influenced by popular music. "Songs are often stitched together into a medley by improvisational playing and modulation to create a sense of seamlessness, of one song flowing into the next."[121]

Music presentation in services have moved to free-flowing praise filled with invitation, engagement, exaltation, adoration, and intimacy. They are services that create space for physical expression and freedom during the worship gathering in the church. The intention of it is to advocate participation in worship rather than just listening. These changes have often caused conflict and worship wars to arise in the church. (I discuss this issue further in Chapter 4.) However, the musical focus in worship should never be solely on style and remaining fresh. It should center on reflecting God's glory and fostering unity between generations and cultures.

Worship Presentation

Worship must be handled with vision, leadership, consideration, and attention when planning. The music presented in worship "requires organizational, pastoral, and communication skills outside of the worship services as well."[122] Every part of worship should be considered. No part in worship is insignificant. Everything must

---

[121] Robb Redman. *The Great Worship Awakening: Singing a New Song in the Postmodern Church.* (San Francisco: Jossey-Bass, 2002), 35.

[122] Greg Scheer, *The Art of Worship: A Musician's Guide to Leading Modern Worship* (Grand Rapids, MI: Baker, 2006.), 87.

flow and go hand in hand with earnest consideration and intention. The culture and DNA of the church must be considered.

It is incumbent that those planning worship have a desire and awareness that each worship experience is a dress rehearsal of the worship gathering that will take place in heaven. This is a humbling and huge responsibility on those who are leading. Wisdom, sound judgement, prayer, scriptural foundation, and accountability to each other must be a part of the process so that God is honored and lives are changed.

Change is sometimes slow and gradual. Yet it can also be rapid and dramatic. However, churches must never be found guilty trying to "fit in" by watering down biblical principles and implementing new methods that have not been effectively evaluated, assessed, or planned. Each section in this chapter has helped to ensure that intentional boundaries for this ministry project and direction for effective worship in an evolving Christian Church will be set. It also set up for the next chapter, which will build upon the set foundation for this project from an exhaustive literary research harmonizing with the purpose and direction of this ministry project.

CHAPTER FOUR

Literature Review

This chapter uncovers a range of relevant sources that have contributed to my research and creation of my ministry project. The purpose of this project is to develop an inclusive worship gathering for The Church of the Living God, Temple #203 and community. In order for this project to be successful, research on the worship practices of Temple #203, as well as what is being practiced in the larger Christian culture, be done. I was able to find substantial literature that I could glean from, embrace, and be nurtured by in order to move toward my goal.

I have concluded from my research that having a clear understanding of worship and the practices of it was vital. It is impossible to effectively fulfill the needs of every generation in any worship experience without having understanding of the main topic. In this chapter is a comprehensive review of some of the literature which include various books, journals, dissertations, and articles that have informed me on this topic and influenced how I decided to go about constructing this ministry project. The resources have been placed under three main areas:

Community and Ministry Setting, Ecclesiological and Theological Foundations, and Research and Design of Program for this Project

COMMUNITY AND CHURCH SETTING

There are many traditions of humankind, cultural identity, doctrines, theologies, interpretations and desired worship styles. They have all contributed to division, the split in Christianity of numerous denominations, worship wars, wounded leaders, and broken communities in the Christian Church. This section has resources that bring focus to the importance of worship in a religious corporate setting with the goal of impacting the larger community.

There is a growing trend of people who have either left the institutional church or have chosen to be religiously unaffiliated. According to Pew Research Center Polling, the highest percentage where that decline is taking place is found in adults 30 and under.[123] Religious importance in that generation has decreased. In the ministry setting for my project, Church of the Living God Temple #203's religious practices and beliefs are Christian.

The community that surrounds this ministry setting is around 51% Christian. However, cultural pressures have plagued the effectiveness of the church in that community. Some feel that the church is more concerned about money, power, rules, and politics rather than it being a house of worship and refuge. Others feel that the church does not help them grow spiritually and religion does not fit into their lifestyle.[124] The resources in this section helped to deal with this reality that is continuing to increase and be visible in many churches, including Temple #203.

The attendance in corporate worship is continuing to decline. In Reggie McNeal's book *Present Future: Six Tough Questions for the Church*, he speaks to the trending realities that the church is not addressing. He provided six realities that the church must consider in order to be effective in an evolving culture where worship attendance is decreasing. These realities are

---

[123] Masci, David. "'Nones' on the Rise." *Pew Research Center's Religion & Public Life Project*. October 09, 2012. Accessed April 18, 2019 from http://www.pewforum.org/

[124] Reggie McNeal, *Present Future: Six Tough Questions for the Church* (Hoboken, NJ: John Wiley & Sons, 2003), 4.

1. The Collapse of the Church Culture
2. The Shift from Church Growth to Kingdom Growth
3. A New Reformation: Releasing God's People
4. The Return to Spiritual Formation
5. The Shift from Planning to Preparation
6. The Rise of Apostolic Leadership

With the decline that is taking place in the church, one of the key areas that that I found beneficial is under the chapter "New Reality Number Five: The Shift from Planning to Preparation." Preparation helps to shape our perspective into a place of readiness for what is ahead. That is what culture has done. Preparing conditions for the future. That seems to be the issue of the church. The church is focused more on planning rather than preparation for the future. Therefore, fresh practices in worship must be done and the historic traditions of the church need to be shaken. Worship is the means where people connect with God and each other.

You cannot prepare without adequate knowledge and education on what is needed in this present culture in worship. Worship is more than just a program in the life of the church on Sundays. Mankind was created to worship, and God wants us to do it in spirit and truth according to John 4:24. However, it is difficult to respond and lead in spirit and truth without knowing the truth about worship.

Gary Mathena contended that anyone who is leading in any area of worship must have a basic knowledge of the historical and biblical foundations of worship. In his book *One Thing Needful: An Invitation to the Study of Worship*, he argues worship done today has been built upon the heritage of worship which includes the early church, medieval church, the Reformation era, modern Protestant worship, and many contemporary worship cultures.[125] With the evolution of culture, leaders have to have more education and be more knowledgeable. They are valued assets for what is ahead. With it, appreciation and comprehension of the purpose and role that

---

[125] Gary M. Mathena, *One Thing Needful: An Invitation to the Study of Worship* (Bloomington, IN: CrossBooks, 2013), xiv.

music and the arts have biblically and historically in worship are grasped.

Mathena discussed seven worship study disciplines which include Introduction to Worship, Theology of Worship, History of Worship, Tabernacle Worship, Music and Worship, the Heart of the Worship Leader, and Lifestyle Worship. I found that these seven disciplines were beneficial to my topic and ministry project. I found no limitations on the topic of worship. He gave an exhaustive study through different topics on worship that also included some biblical and professional insight. This resource caused me to have a deeper level of discipline and understanding on worship so that I would be able to teach effectively and influence during my ministry project.

When worship is not properly planned it will be ineffective. Vernon Whaley provided practical insight on how to plan an effective corporate worship experience in his book *The Dynamics of Corporate Worship*. The information he provided in this book has been broken into three distinct sections: biblical definitions, examples of worship, and useful strategies for planning corporate worship.

Throughout the book, Whaley provided some theological and biblical commentary. In his commentary, he argued that one of the reasons why corporate worship has become ineffective is because of the "pride, arrogance, and selfishness"[126] of those leading in worship. This resource is one of the books that I used in Graduate School for my Masters degree. Therefore, I do not feel that there was any limitation in it. I gravitated to this resource because the content was exceptional for my personal reflection. It also gave tools to properly plan effective corporate worship experiences. I say effective because each aspect of worship that he provided built off of each other with the intent to promote nurturing, developing, and cultivation of our relationship with Him in corporate worship experiences.[127]

---

[126] Vernon M. Whaley, *The Dynamics of Corporate Worship* (Virginia Beach, VA: Academx Publishing Services, 2009), 21.

[127] Ibid., 62.

An effective corporate worship experience has power to draw and influence believers and non-believers with the right music. In Sally Morgenthaler's book *Worship Evangelism: Inviting Unbelievers into the Presence of God*, she speaks to this truth by stressing an importance of combining the best of traditional and contemporary musical practices in one worship service to make it inclusive for Christians and even non-Christians. Morgenthaler noted that there is a negative key change in attitudes concerning the average churchgoer. Going to church has become less to do with an experience with God, which is the original inten,t and now has less to do with God. Worship has become a more market-driven activity for the church-going consumer.[128] This is an unfortunate reality. The church has a greater focus on consumption rather than worshipping.

The average leader of a church desires growth. Focus on a consumer-driven culture disengages the leader from their actual mission. I firmly believe that trying to be competitive and relevant in worship without the presence of authenticity will cause non-believers to continue to feel empty. Authenticity in worship transforms lives and encourages people to be more Christ-like. In other words, "quality must precede quantity."[129] She gave a comprehensive biblical analysis that included a study guide that I was able use as a model for the surveys, group discussions, and information for my ministry project. I did not find many limitations in this book. When I chose this resource, I was looking for answers on what kind of music is best to be presented in worship.

A worship service cannot be transformative in the lives of people without proper planning. In Ed Stetzer and Thom S. Rainer's book *Transformational Church*, they teach leaders how to be more effective in meeting their goals as well as converting vision into reality. "When God transforms lives, He doesn't just build temples of the Holy Spirit in individuals, He builds His church by adding more lives to the

---

[128] Sally Morgenthaler, *Worship Evangelism: Inviting Unbelievers into the Presence of God* (Grand Rapids, MI: Zondervan, 1999), 18.

[129] Ibid., 18.

body."[130] Intentional planning harmonized with prepared worship are powerful tools that God uses to foster transformation and growth in a church and community.

There are three principles that I took away from this resource that helped shape this ministry project. When preparing worship, picking music styles and being intentional about what we desire to achieve in worship fosters people to live like Christ, churches acting like the Body of Christ, and communities impacted by the Kingdom of God.[131] My passion is to see God transform churches and communities. Worship has always been the means for me to achieve that goal.

Many churches have become adapted to being stagnate rather than pushing to become transformative. Stetzer and Rainer gave an overall picture of how powerful the church can be through the message of hope which can be communicated with relative and inclusive worship. This book had no limitations to it. Every part of the authors' arguments had biblical backup. It was filled with passion. It intensified the passion that I have for this ministry project and in my personal ministry as well.

The literature in this section helped to bring greater clarity to the purpose and passion behind this ministry project. Clear understanding of worship, how it operates in the church, and the power it has beyond the church was grasped from the resources in this section. Knowing how the church and community fits and will benefit from worship is key.

Ecclesiological and Theological Foundations

In this section is literature that I found that offers theological and ecclesiological foundations to help govern and influence this ministry project. Before getting deeper into that, I had to get a

---

[130] Ed Stetzer & Thom S. Rainer, *Transformational Church* (Nashville, TN: B&H Publishing, 2010), 1.

[131] Ibid., 1.

better understanding of what these two foundations are. According to Alan Cairns in the *Dictionary of Theological Terms*, the word "ecclesiological" deals with the nature, theology, and structure of the Christian church. "Theology" focuses on the condition of humanity and what God has to say through the facts of Scripture and spiritual illumination about creation.[132] Both of these foundations influenced my perspective on what and how worship should be carried out in the church and community.

In order for one to grasp the information being studied, one must have a grasp of the discipline to even understand the introductory issues that are found in theology books and biblical commentaries.[133] However, many twenty-first century worship leaders will not expend a lot of time reading medieval books about God. M. James Sawyer's provided a more simplified version to be able to study theology in his book, *The Survivor's Guide to Theology.*

Worship has its own theology. In order to effectively lead in worship and create a purposeful ministry project, I knew that I must increase my understanding about God and learn to appreciate Him more as creator. Whether leading through music or in any other capacity of worship, one must be a theologian. Worship leaders communicate the truth about God and assume the responsibility of making sure that God is tangible in worship. Sawyer's book provides theological studies from different scholars, denominations, and religious interpretations. What is presented in this book helps to position the worship and ministry of Temple #203 in the larger Christian World.

Knowing God also includes being conscious of His expectations for humanity. In *The Purpose of Man*, A. W. Tozer invites readers to understand the purpose of worship as well for man to pursue a more intimate relationship with God. "Worship is man's full reason for existence. Worship is why we are born and why we are born

---

[132] Millard J. Erickson, *Christian Theology* (Grand Rapids, MI: Baker Academic, 2013), 8.

[133] M. James Sawyer, *The Survivor's Guide to Theology* (Grand Rapids, MI: Zondervan, 2006), 10.

again."[134] From that understanding, we find that worship is a part of our created expectation on this earth.

Harold Best's explanation in an upcoming resource concerning worship is very similar to Tozer's. The difference between Best and Tozer is Tozer says that worship is our reason for breathing.[135] Best states that we were created worshiping.[136] From Tozer's view about worship, I concluded that he felt that we are wasting away in life if we do not worship. This also comes from a man who was ambitious about loving God more than anyone of his generation. I interpreted from the words of Best that worship is not a choice to be made.

This book was filled with wisdom with no limitations of biblical insight. He did a remarkable job presenting his case concerning God's created purpose for mankind. One scripture reference that Tozer pointed out is Psalm 40:3. Psalm 40:3 says, "He put a new song in my mouth, a hymn of praise to our God. Many will see and fear and put their trust in the Lord." Worship is a continuous outpouring that must continue to be renewed. We must continuously seek God for new and brilliant ways to enrich the corporate worship experience.[137]

This book took me through a worship journey that ignited my passion to influence others through this project. It must be clear that leaders must develop the heart, fire, and passion to worship God without limitation. Otherwise, we cannot lead where we have never been and do not believe. Worship is "the true healing water for the wounded souls of religious men."[138] Worship inspires our testimony. Worship changes our lives internally and externally. God's wonders and mercies are witnessed through and because of worship. Worship

---

[134] A.W. Tozer, *The Purpose of Man* (Ventura, CA: Regal, 2009), 29.

[135] Ibid., 29.

[136] Harold M. Best, *Unceasing Worship: Biblical Perspectives on Worship and the Arts* (Downers Grove, IL: InterVarsity Press, 2003), 17.

[137] Ibid., 11.

[138] A.W. Tozer, *The Purpose of Man* (Ventura, CA: Regal, 2009), 73.

should not drive people away from God. Also, it should never be an afterthought if we plan to be effective serving multi-generations, multi-ethnicities, and multi-cultures. Therefore, music in worship must be more than some performance we do, but a presence we experience.[139]

Worship is our created responsibility. Harold M. Best concluded in his book, *Unceasing Worship: Biblical Perspectives on Worship and the Arts*, that we have not been created for or to worship. We have been created worshipping.[140] Worship is not a choice according to Best. We were created doing it. The issue is that our worship has become idle and misguided. His conclusion comes from the Genesis of all creation.

We have been created in God's image. Worship is a part of our imputed nature. We are continuous and relentless beings that need to worship.[141] Our created nature makes us pour ourselves in directions that either worships God or false gods. This is a very different approach than most of the resources provided in this chapter. Most of the resources suggest that worship is a decision and choice. However, argues differently that we have been created to worship, but our worship has been misguided by the many distractions of culture.

Best concluded that there is a staleness in worship. This staleness is not only in the church, but in our personal lives. He said that worship is not a complex specialty but should be a common practice.[142] Leaders have to continuously seek for a freshness in our witnessing, preaching, prayer, teaching, imagining, crafting, and in the arts.[143] It has to start within us before projecting it to the church and community. There is no limitation of wisdom in this book.

---

[139] Ibid., 177.

[140] Harold M. Best, *Unceasing Worship: Biblical Perspectives on Worship and the Arts* (Downers Grove, IL: InterVarsity Press, 2003), 18.

[141] Ibid., 19.

[142] Ibid.., 11.

[143] Ibid, 11.

Worship must be a continuous pursuit to please a perfect God rather than trying to please ourselves. In Greg McCabe's book *Biblical Worship: Pursuing Intimacy with God*, he challenges our ways of thinking in this present culture about worship. Worship in too many churches has become filled with too much "I" (selfishness, self-love, self-glory, and self-fulfillment) and not enough "C" (Christ).[144] Worship has also become more about where people live, ethnicity, and culture[145] which is the fuel of worship wars, splits, and division in the Church community. They have interfered with our ability to have a personal relationship with God and to effectively lead others in that direction.

We cannot lead others without clarity and understanding where we went wrong. Scripture reminds us in Proverbs 4:7 that we must get understanding before development and pursuit of anything. The wisdom in this resource provided increased clarity concerning God's heart and how we must connect with his. The only limitation of this book is it did not discuss any musical aspects of worship that would benefit this ministry project. However, the content from this resource is still sufficient information for my ministry project.

Genuine worship must have biblical motivation; otherwise, it can be offensive to God. In C. John Collin's journal *An Idiomatic Proposal*, he does a short biblical exposition on John 4:23-24. In this article he proposed that the context of this passage is more complex than God requiring two independent elements to our worship. Truth conveys the idea of genuineness that involves actions. Spirit relates to the inner man. Paul says in Romans 1:9, "I worship God in my spirit." This clarifies that in spirit is the location where God is more concerned about where He is to be worshipped.[146]

Collins provides a very concise contribution to this passage

---

[144] Greg McCabe, *Biblical Worship: Pursuing Intimacy with God* (Bloomington, IN: WestBow Press, 2015), Introduction.

[145] Ibid., Introduction.

[146] C John Collins, "John 4:23-24, 'In Sprit and Truth': An Idiomatic Proposal." *Presbyterian* 21 no. 2 (1995): 120.

of scripture. There is no limitation to biblical commentary and exegesis. This journal helps to grab a better understanding of the topic of worship for my ministry project. Jesus said to the Samaritan woman that genuine worshippers will choose to worship in their inner self, their minds, their feelings, and in their activities.[147] When we know better, it is easier to facilitate from a place of clarity and understanding.

Many argue that the Old Testament is not relevant for New Testament believers. In A. E. Hill's book *Enter His Courts with Praise!: Old Testament Worship for the New Testament Church*, he provides a study on what the Old Testament has to say about worship renewal in the church. Hill taught New Testament believers how worship should be expressed, when, where, the artistry should be incorporated, done, our actions, and the different rituals from an Old Testament perspective. This resource is filled with biblical interpretation and illustrations from Scripture.

For example, in the Old Testament, the idol gods of the people became a real threat to exclusive worship to the one true living God.[148] There was constant tension and confrontation between Moses and the magicians of Pharaoh. The magicians tried to replicate what was divine by using religious systems that energized demonic forces.[149] Our energy, our worship, our song must be unto God not gods. In Exodus 15:2, Moses says that Jehovah is the subject matter and inspiration of our song.[150]

This book promotes a fresh and meaningful worship for the emerging church in an evolving worship. The content of this book

---

[147] Ibid., 121.

[148] A E. Hill, *Enter His Courts with Praise!: Old Testament Worship for the New Testament Church* (Grand Rapids, MI: Baker, 1993), xxv.

[149] Ibid., xxv.

[150] Lange, Johann Peter, Tayler Lewis, A. Gosman, Mead, Charles Marsh, ; 1836-1911. ; Exodus, Or, The Second Book of Moses, and Gardiner, Frederic, ; 1822-1889. ; Leviticus, Or, The Third Book of Moses. *Commentary on the Holy Scriptures: Critical, Doctrinal and Homiletical.* (Grand Rapid, MI: Zondervan, 1960), 53.

does not lack any biblical, historical, or theological foundation. It is very comprehensive and exhaustive by providing answers to the many questions that even include our vocabulary to be used in worship. There was no limitation to how detailed he became concerning worship. Words reflect the totality of a person's nature and character at the human level. This means that our words reveal our motives, personality, and character.[151] Insight like these influences what we say, do, and allow to be sung as we enter into His courts with praise.

The old traditions should never be erased; they are qualifiers for the new. In Robert E. Webber's book *Worship Old and New,* he challenged the readers by arguing that we should not get rid of the old traditions. We should build a worship that respects the old traditions but having an awareness and seek new ways to incorporate new methods in the contemporary church.[152] This is very important for the ministry setting of this ministry project that has a strong traditional heritage that comes out of the experience and denomination of the people in the church. However, the desire is to find ways to be effectively relevant for all generations.

Webber postured his argument by providing three interrelated explanations concerning worship in many churches around the world. They are "1) Churches of nearly every tradition are discovering the worship of the biblical and historical traditions. 2) Churches of nearly every denomination are discovering each other and area recognizing that elements of worship preserved in other traditions are relevant to today's worship. 3) What is happening is the convergence of worship traditions, a blending of worship old and new."[153]

It is very important to have a balance in worship and that balance must be presented in my ministry project. The old and new styles of music for worship must be presented in this project. Also, there must

---

[151] A E. Hill, *Enter His Courts with Praise!: Old Testament Worship for the New Testament Church* (Grand Rapids, MI: Baker, 1993), 2.

[152] Robert E. Webber, *Worship Old and New* (Grand Rapids, MI: Zondervan, 1994), 13.

[153] Ibid., 12.

be liturgical balance in worship. In essence, worship should have options. In order for worship to be authentic and fulfilling for each generation, a blended style of worship seems to be the most fruitful style that will not only attract but keep people in church. Webber does a great job finding a way to preserve the best of the past while walking in confidence into the future.[154]

These resources made it even more clear to me that the imperfections of worship have a lot to do with the inconsistencies of our humanity. Our worship must be guided so that we will lead and practice what is acceptable to God. Worship should not be like a lottery that we take a chance upon weekly, hoping to feel His presence. If so, "we lose the power and stabilizing guarantees of Scripture."[155] The resources in this section not only deal with our individual perspectives of worship, they help to find ways for renewal in our corporate settings.

RESEARCH AND/OR PROGRAM DESIGN

This final section provides more contemporary resources that help bring character and conclusion to the development of my ministry project. Greater input about worship wars and how we transition from them to a more effective worship format will be in this section. Worship must become more substantive and musically inclusive.

Every song does not work for every kind of church in worship. In Dawn's article Beyond the Worship Wars," she addresses worship wars, challenges in planning worship, and being able to judge what is substantive and effective music for worship. Many congregations find themselves fighting over what style of music to use in worship.[156] However, when planning worship, it must be able to answer critical questions that Dawn provided. They are

---

[154] Ibid., 15.

[155] Ibid., 51.

[156] Marva J. Dawn, "Beyond the Worship Wars" *Christian Century* (June 4-11, 1997), 550.

1. What kind of people are being formed by our worship practices?
2. How will worship equip us for mission throughout the week?
3. What will bring us together as a community?[157]

These are some very critical questions that she asked. If worship does not contribute to growth in our relationship with God, nurture our personal character, and the development of our community, then we have not met our goal in worship.[158] We are simply going through religious motions. Although this article addressed several things, it did not have any limitations concerning the matter at hand, appropriate music in worship. With those critical questions, I found it necessary that this ministry project must have sound instruction, direction, and wisdom for the ministry setting to find music that is balanced and suitable for their church. Dawn's article helped me conclude that the music in worship must be inviting and hospitable to outsiders who may be strangers in the corporate setting of worship.

Balanced music presented in worship has the power to draw people to Christ. In Tamara J. Van Dyken's article, "Worship Wars, Gospel Hymns, and Cultural Engagement in American Evangelicalism, 1890 – 1940" noted that worship music was essential to the negotiation between what is considered churchy tradition and practical faith, between institutional authority and popular choice.[159] Therefore, from her assessment, she concluded that music influences evangelism. This is reminiscent of Morgenthaler's conclusion. Worship and evangelism go hand in hand.[160] Therefore, in order to compete with an increasingly secular mainstream culture, mass

---

[157] Ibid., 550.

[158] Ibid., 550.

[159] Tamara J. Van Dyken, "Worship Wars, Gospel Hymns, and Cultural Engagement in American Evangelicalism, 1890 – 1940" *Religion and American Culture: A Journal of Interpretation* 27 no. 2 (2017): 192.

[160] Sally Morgenthaler, *Worship Evangelism: Inviting Unbelievers into the Presence of God* (Grand Rapids, MI: Zondervan, 1999), 77.

appeal in the area of music is essential. [161] Worship draws people to Christ.

Dyken provided historical information that highlights the worship wars that have taken place in the church over time. Worship wars have not ceased in the church. They are still evident in the modern church today. The battles between traditional hymnals and gospel music continues to be a struggle. However, what has divided churches could really bring churches together. Music style is central to uniting generations, communities, believers, and non-believers in the American Protestant Churches in this century.[162] However, it must be done effectively. It is very crucial in the life of worship; otherwise, the pews will continue to empty.

Diverse music is essential to a growing church. In Soong Chan Rah's book *Many Colors: Cultural Intelligence for a Changing Church,* he surveyed multiple ethnicities, churches, and communities to see how culture affects an evolving church. The benefit of his survey is it showed me that I need to do the same. Doing a survey for my research project will be beneficial because it delivers more accurate and targeted results to help me assess and make strategic decisions of what is needed informatively for my ministry project.

Collecting information from diverse individuals give diverse perspectives upon how worship has become ineffective in Temple #203. Diversity is not limited to generations. Diversity should also be assessed ethnically. Rah said, "There is a burgeoning movement of multiethnic congregations in the United States."[163] Temple #203 has multiple ethnicities in their community. In an effort to be culturally sensitive and inclusive, this is one area that should lifted for consideration. I do not expect for this church to change its

---

[161] Ibid., 192.

[162] Tamara J. Van Dyken, "Worship Wars, Gospel Hymns, and Cultural Engagement in American Evangelicalism, 1890 – 1940" *Religion and American Culture: A Journal of Interpretation,* 27 no. 2 (2017), 191.

[163] Soong Chan Rah. *Many Colors: Cultural Intelligence for a Changing Church.* (Chicago: Moody Publishers, 2010), 11.

ethnic dynamics. However, it is worth at least discussing it during the ministry project.

Many books address the cultural differences in the world. However, in the context of the church, communicating God's truth to an evolving society can be challenging. Rah gave an exhaustive biblical contribution to this topic. It does not deal with worship and how it has the power to unify cultures and ethnicities in the church, but this is a needed resource that can widen the lens of Temple #203.

While the church is striving to be relevant it must be careful that casualties do not occur while doing so. In Dave Williamson's book *God's Singers: A Guidebook for the Worship Leading Choir in the 21st Century,* he brought up one of the major casualties that have taken place throughout the worship wars in the church. That issue is the dismantling of choirs and shifting to ensembles in order to create a more contemporary look and sound. This issue has brought about controversy in the church. It creates silo groups where not only the music has become exclusive in a church, but singers have become exclusive, like an elite group that is independent of the rest of the music department.

Williamson suggested a concept of creating a Worship Leading Choir.[164] This is a positive direction that continues to allow the many gifts that are in the church to be used in worship. A worship leading choir performs relevant, diverse sounds, different styles of music, and serves in diverse formats of worship. In each chapter, Williamson gives a step-by-step process on how to build this type of choir.

This prescription could change a ministry's decision from getting rid of the choir and moving to an ensemble. One of the strengths of this resource is the writer not only provided biblical research, but hands-on research from many ministry settings. Therefore, I chose to include the chart that is provided in this book to strengthen my stance that removal of the church choir is a horrible move by any church.

---

[164] Dave Williamson, *God's Singers: A Guidebook for the Worship Leading Choir in the 21st Century* (Baton Rouge, LA: In:cite Media, 2010), 111.

Worship Leading Choir Paradigms Chart

Table 4.1

Outward Signs

TRADITIONAL CHOIR	WORSHIP LEADING CHOIR
Sings horizontally to the people	Songs vertically to the Lord
Practical role: Spiritual Entertainers	Practical role: Lead Worshipers
Performs for Jesus	Worships for Jesus
Celebrates the Gift of music	Celebrates the Giver
Hopes to hear "You can great"	Hopes to hear "God is great"
Has a minor impact	Has a major impact
Engenders emotion for the moment	Engenders significance for eternity

Table 4.2

Inward Signs

TRADITIONAL CHOIR	WORSHIP LEADING CHOIR
Partners in singing	Partners in worship and ministry
Acquaintances	Family
Competitors	Fellow servants
Basically bored	Primarily passion
Director: Music professor	Director: pastor, coach, cheerleader
Searches for talented members	Searches for faithful members[165]

This chart is just an example of the content that is presented inside this book. It shows that there are tangible solutions that can be looked at when seeking ideas for change and improvement in the music department of the worship ministry. The effectiveness of the music ministry in worship is a large component for this ministry project.

Musicians must be skilled and anointed; they have the power to control the atmosphere in worship. In Greg Scheer's book *The Art of Worship: A Musician's Guide to Leading Modern Worship,* he offers help for churches when they are trying to hire a musician as well as what to look for in the music program of the worship ministry. The focus in

---

[165] Ibid., 56.

this book is on the musicians rather than singers as in Williamson's book. Scheer is an experienced, professional musician with academic credentials that make him a great resource for this topic.

I personally have served in leadership for various music ministries at several churches for almost 30 years. It is easy after a period of time to become complacent and creativity can become "out-of-date." Many musicians who are older find themselves going through that challenge. Scheer provided valuable insight from his professional experience that is worth applying and assessing during the development of this project. My plan is to incorporate some of these suggestions in my ministry project. Briefly, some of them are

1. During a trial period, get feedback from those in the congregation rather than just perceiving that they value the changes made in the music and worship style.
2. Do not be upset if the new worship expressions fail. It is a part of the process.
3. Build slowly. The ultimate goal is to help people worship in spirit and truth, not to become the hippest church in the shortest amount of time.
4. Focused funding for architecture, sound, personnel, etc. for worship is appropriate.
5. Adapt to new structures and styles of worship. When styles of music change, it may benefit to explore other worship formats.
6. Be detailed and intentional with the music that will presented in worship.[166]

More biblical insights could have been offered. But I wasn't necessarily looking for biblical insight out of this resource. Scheer offered the insight of a music professional. In my words, everything that needs to be taught and learned isn't always spiritual. Having a needed degree of skill set as a leader in worship should be a

---

[166] Greg Scheer, *The Art of Worship: A Musician's Guide to Leading Modern Worship* (Grand Rapids, MI: Baker, 2006), 26-30.

requirement that cannot be overlooked. What he provided out of his vocation and calling is a rich ingredient to the purpose of this ministry project.

The methods of worship must be assessed often, or ministries will find themselves stuck and left behind from culture. In Warren Bird, Ed Stetzer, and Elmer Towns' book *11 Innovations in the Local Church,* they help leaders who serve in the church become uncomfortable by widening their lens to some new innovations to consider in the church. As things are evolving, leaders are being left behind. Culture has changed and our churches have also, but no one has told us! [167] When churches get to the point that they are incapable of reaching multiple generations and they have become lethargic, there is obviously a need for some new innovations.

The innovations that are in this book have been evaluated across churches in America. They have proven to be impactful for multiple generations, cultures, and ethnicities. This resource actually provided me with more ideas to consider for discussion in my project. It is essential that ministries must be free and courageous to change the methods of ministry not the mission. "American churches have become lethargic and have stopped looking for breakthrough. Churches across the country are slowly dying because too many tend to value tradition over expanding God's reach."[168] This is a major argument in this book and issue in the church. The only limitation that this resource has is it does not speak to the music part of worship. However, it sets the barometer for many things where music can be inserted for the new innovations that could possibly change the model and look of the church.

Worship style influences congregational growth in the Christian Church. In Michael Hakmin Lee's journal, *Hallelujah! Worship Style and Congregational Growth,* he argues from research completed through the Billy Graham Center that denominational loyalty has

---

[167]   Warren Bird, Ed Stetzer, and Elmer Towns, *11 Innovations in the Local Church* (Ventura, CA: Regal Books, 2007), foreword.

[168]   Ibid., 14.

eroded and been replaced by music style.[169] The significance of music style with a congregation's reach and numerical growth has a lot to do with the level of the music ministry that matches who the church is trying to target. He said, "you must match your music to the kind of people God wants your church to reach."[170]

Lee's survey and research provided clear findings of why churches that have a more contemporary worship and musical style are growing. The journal provided insight but lacked biblical commentary and theological insight. However, the elements of research done, along with the information provided will be vital components that includes four tables. Each table gives percentages of growth and decline from different congregations. Also, how music and different innovations make a significant difference in the growth of a church. This journal helps makes more evident what my ministry project is projecting more tangible and visible.

Congregations are struggling because they have not embraced the lessons from the past. In Robb Redman's book *The Great Worship Awakening: Singing a New Song in the Postmodern Church*, highlighted four major developments in the Christian worship trends. These trends are The Seeker Service Movement, the Praise and Worship Movement, the Christian Worship Music Industry, and the Liturgical Renewal Movement. Each movement has lessons that can be taught to struggling congregations who are considering change in their worship music and format. There are important social and cultural insights that affect the pace of change, ethnic and cultural diversity, generational dynamics, the emerging postmodern worldview, emphasis on personal experience, popular culture, and new communication media and information technology.[171]

---

[169] Michael Hakmin Lee, "Hallelujah! Worship Style and Congregational Growth" *Choral Journal* (November 2017): 67.

[170] Ibid., 67.

[171] Robb Redman, *The Great Worship Awakening: Singing a New Song in the Postmodern Church.* (San Francisco: Jossey-Bass, 2002), xii.

These are some very important features for congregations who are battling with preservation of their worship heritage while trying to become relevant in their worship. Nothing like change in worship creates the greatest tension and conflict in a church.[172]

Redman helped me to continue to find ways to implement strategy and ways of promoting change in a ministry setting that is intentional on preserving their worship heritage and liturgical format. The history that Redman provided from the four major Christian trends were great to see how worship and music has evolved. There is no limitation to the insight he provided in that area. History is very important because it helps to give clarity and understanding on why things are the way they are. Also, we are able to learn from the mistakes of the former.

Redman was intentional in providing a pathway for music ministries to promote an awakening in the culture of their church. This is one of the goals for Temple #203. I want to promote an awakening that will make this ministry setting aware of the endless possibilities and power that the renewal of music in worship possesses. In the words of Redman, "suggest helpful ways of responding that encourage renewal of worship in an established church."[173] This resource solely focuses on change and that is the primary purpose of my ministry project.

CONCLUSION

The complacency of the church and leadership has become an epidemic that goes beyond the ministry setting for this ministry project. No one has the ability to accurately predict what will be best for the worship patterns in the future. However, after research, it is safe to bet that culture, music, and the needs of people will continue to change. The resources in this chapter are foundational and concrete.

---

[172] Ibid, xiii.

[173] Ibid., xiii.

Thomas Long concluded that we must "hope that the church will be guided toward a deeper faith and a truer worship."[174] The three sections and the literature under each of them in this chapter help to shape renewal, strategy, and biblical insight for an evolving worship ministry needed in the church. The design of this project is to generate movement by building a plan and project that will reveal more of God and create an effective worship ministry. The content from the resources contributed to my overall understanding of what will be used for this ministry project done at Temple #203. The end result will create a lasting change in Temple #203 and its surrounding community for all generations, cultures, and ethnicities.

---

[174] Thomas G. Long.,"Salvos in the Worship Wars," *The Living Pulpit*, January – March 2004, 35.

CHAPTER FIVE

Ministry Project Strategy: Goals and Plans

MINISTRY PROJECT DESIRED OUTCOMES

Preparation for this project began with prayer and vision. Proverbs 20:18 says, "Where vision is absent, people are abandoned." Vision helps to focus our creative thoughts into an organized journey toward intended goals and outcomes. This project is simply that. It is an organized journey that will take my chosen ministry setting on a pathway of change for the music and worship in the church. This project will guide them toward creating an inclusive worship experience for all generations. Exhaustive research, analysis, assessments, surveys, awareness, and spiritual guidance all have aided in the creation of this project.

Vision is not just about answers as much as it is about direction. Leadership offers direction to followers and takes them to a specific destination.[175] Every part of this project has to be led with calculation, clarity, and intention. The intention of this project is to bring multiple generations and cultures together and meet their needs through music

---

[175] Week 9: "*Week 9 Leadership vs. Management*" (online assignment introduction, MIN7560 Person and Practice of Ministry, South University). Accessed August 23, 2019.

in worship. This is not an easy task; however, collaborative insight of volunteers coupled with exhaustive research helped frame this project. Both guide precise decisions and direction for what I conclude will be the best practices for facilitating an inclusive worship experience for every generation and culture in my chosen ministry setting.

This project also promotes growth in multiple areas of the ministry setting for this project. The purpose of any vision is to meet needs. In Proverbs 29:18, vision is translated as "revelation." That word in this particular context was commonly associated with the visions of the prophets and stands for the importance of prophetic exhortation to a community.[176] When trying to achieve harmony, change, growth, or when leading a community in a certain direction, there must be vision or revelation with clarity.

My burden and passion behind this project were birthed from the experiences I had in local churches in surrounding faith communities that are struggling to survive. It has become disheartening as well as discouraging to see churches declining, pastors abandoning churches, ministers who are stressed and struggling, communities falling apart where the church used to thrive, etc. Therefore, my conclusion is that the Christian Church is struggling because they are being left behind in an evolving culture. Churches have become stagnate with no answer of finding ways to move back into a direction of health, growth, and strength.

Many churches in this present age are surviving rather than thriving. Many lack substantive evidence of new life being breathed into the church. Worship services have become rudimentary and complacent with no direction. Many churches have tried to facilitate modernized change in their worship services; however, ineffective implementation of those changes has caused greater challenges. Challenges that are ultimately revealed in the decline of attendance in worship services. This could be avoided when there is proper planning before implementation.

---

[176] Duane A. Garrett. *The New American Commentary*. Vol. 14. Proverbs, Ecclesiastes, Song of Songs. (Nashville, TN: Broadman & Holman, 1997), Proverbs 29:18.

Some stunning statistics have shown "sixty to eighty percent of young people will leave the church in their twenties."[177] They will not come back until they have experienced some type of crisis or later in life. The Barna Research Group surveyed that there are about 300,000 Protestant churches in America.[178] Kevin Brosius stated that only 15 percent of churches in America are growing. Only 2 to 5 percent of those churches are experiencing what can be called "new conversion" growth while the others are experiencing "transferred growth."[179]

Transferred growth is where the bigger churches are receiving members from other churches and the smaller churches are closing down all together.[180] The focus of this ministry project is intentional on focusing on providing an avenue through worship for my chosen ministry setting to experience "new conversion growth" rather than the other. This project will create an energetic push by creating a worship experience format that will include a musical style that will fit the worship culture for the church and community. It will help sustain those who are present in the church and promote new conversion growth.

KEY THEOLOGICAL CONCLUSIONS AND RATIONAL FOR THE CREATION OF THE PROGRAM

Previous research and assessments of multiple denominations and churches reveal that there are imploding conflicts continuing to happen in the Christian Church. In Tamara Dyken's article, "Worship Wars, Gospel Hymns and Cultural Engagement in American

---

[177] David Kinnaman, *You Lost Me: Why Young Christians Are Leaving Church and Rethinking Faith* (Grand Rapids, MI: Baker, 2011).

[178] "Is there a 'Reformed' Movement in American Churches?" Barna Group, November 15, 2010. Accessed July 13, 2019 from https://www.barna.com/

[179] Kevin Brosius, "Culture and the Church's Discipleship Strategy" *The Journal of Ministry & Theology*, 124-125.

[180] Jim Putman, *Church Is a Team Sport: A Championship Strategy for Doing Ministry Together* (Grand Rapids, MI: Baker Books, 2008), 71.

Evangelicalism," it was made clear that the worship wars that took place in the church have disunited generations, communities, believers, and non-believers. The desire to maintain a traditional worship culture and style that reflects the religious heritage of the former has a lot to do with the splits in the Christian Church.

It is argued that the effectiveness of the past religious practices should still be effective in the present age. They are suitable for faith development of believers and new believers. There is some truth to that argument. However, the belief that the old ways will renew the church is a belief that is difficult to reach. Many believe that the historic religious practices of the church will thrive again. I strongly disagree with this belief. The churches that are holding onto that mindset have caused the Christian Church to be contaminated with continuous worship wars because they choose to disregard what is taking place in an evolving culture.

Kieran Flanagan, a sociologist from Great Britain, concluded that something has changed in the way the liturgy is presented in the Catholic Church, perhaps even a change in attitude on the part of the celebrant and the congregation.[181] There can be an even balance between excitement and sacredness in worship. Those who lead and those who follow should be able to assemble themselves in concert to worship God. Worship should reflect the words of David in Psalm 122:1, "I was glad whey they said unto me, "Let us go into the house of the Lord." It is God's will that we unite with excitement in worship together.

It is difficult to find excitement where chaos, tension, and struggle exist. Many churches have tried to move away from the older, more familiar and possibly more 'sacred' music and have attempted to gravitate towards modern instrumentation, pop-based formats and the intrusion of the decidedly 'profane' into Christian worship.[182] This is more visible in the evangelical and free churches.

---

[181] Thomas Wagner, Carolyn Landau, and Monique Marie Ingalls, *Christian Congregational Music: Performance, Identity and Experience.* Congregational Music Studies Series (England: Routledge, 2013), 170.

[182] Ibid., 170.

Recently I saw multiple videos of older congregations trying to arrange popular R & B music into sacred worship music with the intended effort to meet and reach younger generations. This is another example of when implementing culture into worship is ineffective. The younger generations who were in the congregation seemed more entertained from the performance of the 60-70-year-old singers and musicians who performing popular secular music in worship. However, the motives and intentions of the older generation were not to entertain. It was to reach and appeal to the younger generations in effort to bring them closer to God.

The authenticity of the efforts and motives of the older generations was lost and drowned in the entertainment and performance of the music. I can even see where the attempts made could have been viewed as offensive, depending upon where one may be in the walk with Christ. Offense keeps us from fulfilling God's purpose. I understand that we must become all things to all people in order to save some. (1 Cor 9:19-23). However, I also believe that the message was drowned in their presentation. It was another attempt to reach younger generations that was ineffectively implemented. Any church that continues to unsuccessfully implement innovations of culture in worship will find themselves continuing to struggle to survive while those who effectively plan, and implement will thrive.

Reggie McNeal observed, "The church culture in North America is a vestige of the original movement, an institutional expression of religion that is in part a civil religion and in part a club where religious people can hang out with other people whose politics, worldview and lifestyles match theirs."[183] As time moves forward, politics, worldviews, and lifestyles will continue to evolve. It is necessary that the worship expressions in the church mirror the same. Worship is at the center of every church's life. Scripture admonishes that we "teach, admonish one another in psalms and hymns and spiritual songs, singing with thankfulness in our hearts to God," (Col 3:16-17). It provides opportunity to reach a mass amount of people at one time

---

[183] Reggie, McNeal. *Present Future: Six Tough Questions for the Church* (Hoboken, NJ: John Wiley & Sons, 2003), 1.

on a week-to-week basis.[184] God is honored and lives are changed at the same time. However, the music done in worship has the power to influence the church positively or negatively.

Next to theology, music has the highest honor concerning the expressions in worship.[185] Music is cultural and stylistic. It has the ability to connect with multiple races, ages, and cultures in the church more than any other expression in worship. Whatever style of music is chosen, it must always direct people toward obedience, unity, maturity, and healing. It should never be used as a tool of entertainment. Music in worship must always be directional toward God. It is in worship that we "sing to him and tell about His wondrous works," (Ps 105:2). The sound of music in worship must always foster biblical foundation that reflect the glory of God.

Churches have been found guilty of syncretism without knowledge that they are even doing it. Being relevant should never remove biblical foundation to be relevant with culture. The right music in worship will release an encounter with God that will cause repentance, redemption, relationship, regeneration, and restoration corporately and individually. Cultural relevance in music only encourages methodical change, not the message of Christ. Worship music must never lose critical and basic elements of the Gospel when attempting to adapt with culture. Otherwise it will reflect the nature of man and desires of man rather than focus on glorifying God.

One of the most important topics on the lips of the pastor, worship leader, and people is worship.[186] There should never be a time when the world is confused about the message of Christ because of the familiarity of secular music being played in the church. The different styles of music in worship must be passionately and intentionally

---

[184] Richard A. Krause, *Worship Wars at the Dawn of a New Millennium:* Lutheranism and the Means of Grace vs. The "Success Story" of American Evangelicalism. (American Theological Library Association, 2016), 164.

[185] Elmer Towns and Vernon Whaley, *Worship Through the Ages.* (Nashville, TN: Broadman and Holman, 2012), 108.

[186] Robert E. Webber. *Worship Old & New.* (Grand Rapids, MI: Zondervan, 1994), 17.

carried out. Scripture says, "Do not love the world nor the things in the world. If anyone loves the world, the love of the Father is not in him," (1 John 2:15). In this epistle, John strongly urged against being aligned with the earthly system that is controlled by the powers of darkness and that has aligned itself against God and his kingdom.[187]

There is a constant battle between darkness and light. Our allegiance must never be divided. There should be a clear difference in worship between the two. Whenever one tries to present music that is culturally inspired, it must be specific and intentionally focused, or it will lose its salty flavor according to scripture. Then the music will become tasteless and no longer good for anything (Matt 5:13). Everything cannot be accepted in worship. Music should be assessed and chosen through education and prayer. Otherwise, any misapplication will lead to calamity and demise.

It has become evident in this world, even the Christian community that humanity has fallen and is being influenced by the powers of evil.[188] The incessant clamoring of culture wars that are continuously waging against the intentions of our spirit have crept their way into places of worship. When dealing with social and cultural issues in the church we must never influence Christians to compromise our beliefs. Compromise in music can influence that mindset. As we seek to implement an effective worship experience in our churches, our decisions must always seek to meet the needs of humanity by seeking first to please God. Scripture tells us to, "seek ye first the kingdom of God and His righteousness, and all these things shall be added to you," (Matt 6:33).

Worship is a gift from God that helps us conform our ways and thoughts toward God's perfect will. The hearts of men cry out to be freed from the continuous battles we face in this life. The passion, urgency of this topic along with the implementation of this project

---

[187] Daniel L. Akin. *The New American Commentary*: 1,2,3, John. Vol. 38 (Nashville, TN: Broadman & Holman, 2001), 1 John 2:15.

[188] Week 1: "*The Problem and the Solution*" (online assignment introduction, MIN7050 Christian Spiritual Formation, South University). Accessed March 3, 2018.

will promote a necessary journey for the ministry setting, the leaders of this church, and potentially the universal church at large. This project is the beginning of a revolutionary journey that will be an ongoing process of development through practices and doctrine.[189] All individuals who serve in leadership must be open minded to the possibilities and the changes ahead.

LEADERS WILL DEVELOP A GREATER APPRECIATION AND UNDERSTANDING FOR DIFFERENT STYLES OF MUSIC IN WORSHIP

In order to move throughout this journey, it has to be facilitated with energetic and effective leadership. The influence of leadership will greatly impact how this journey is carried out. In any organization, leaders must create an environment of productivity, enthusiasm, trust, and growth. Followers are influenced by their leaders' values, quirks, habits, what they communicate, and behaviors.[190] What may seem difficult to implement becomes possible through effective leadership.

In this specific ministry setting, the pastor acknowledged that change was necessary. He was very open to finding answers and gaining insight to what will be the "answer" to helping him move the ministry forward from a worship standpoint. It is very difficult to lead change from a place of ignorance or refusal that there is a need for change.

Being a great leader does not mean that one has the answer. Having a willingness to collaborate with others, a desire to continue to learn, embracing the changes in culture, and expanding their potential as a leader are characteristics of a great leader. When

---

[189] Peter Schineller,"Interculturation and Syncretism: What is the Real Issue?" *International Bulletin of Missionary Research* (February, 1992). Accessed August 11, 2019 from http://www.internationalbulletin.org/issues/1992-02/1992-02-050-schineller.pdf.

[190] John C. Maxwell, *The 360 Leader: Developing Your Influence from Anywhere in the Organization* (Nashville, TN: Thomas Nelson, 2011), 147.

the climate is promoting change but the leader has concluded that learning is no longer an asset for their individual ministry, that organization is headed toward major conflict and disaster. Education qualifies and validates our position as we serve God's people. As I stated in a previous chapter, "leadership and learning are indispensable to each other."[191]

The senior pastor of this ministry setting, Bishop Rex Waddell, first led this journey by his willingness to embrace the realities that were being visible in his church. In Chapter two, I shared candid insights from very transparent interviews that Bishop Waddell and I had. The passion he possessed stimulated greater intensity, excitement, and passion as I prepared for this project and journey. Any further leadership from him after our interviews and conversations had to be aborted. In order for this project not to be compromised, he could not actively promote or lead on any level.

Bishop Waddell's influence and presence during this project could possibly hinder volunteers from being honest about their desires and needs of the worship of the church. The intent of the project is to receive honest assessments and insight from each volunteer who is a current member of this church. The end result is to create an authentic worship format with a balanced style of music. Participation in this project could not be influenced by leaders in the pulpit. It had to be encouraged and announced by lay members of the church. Every approach in preparation for this project had to be strategic.

Effective leadership does not always start and end from the head. Sometimes the greatest influence in the church comes from the second chair, not the first. In John Maxwell's book *360 Degree Leader* and from his other book *21 Irrefutable Laws of Leadership*, he stated that "the true measure of leadership is influence – nothing more, nothing less."[192] This project had to promote participation from lay

---

[191] "JFK Library." Remarks Prepared for Delivery at the Trade Mart in Dallas, TX, November 22, 1963. Accessed May 16, 2019 from https://www.jfklibrary.org/.

[192] John C. Maxwell, *The 360 Leader: Developing Your Influence from Anywhere in the Organization* (Nashville, TN: Thomas Nelson, 2011), 4.

members of the church. They possibly have greater influence in the congregation than the pastor does at times. Their influence could cause reproduction, productivity, and change in a way that seems improbable by first-chair leadership.

There are many different musical styles that can potentially connect with various people in the ministry setting and others that are trying to be caught. Most of the musical worship wars that have happened in the church began with leadership. In other words, there was disagreement between a bureaucrat and vision. The bureaucrat in most situations will choose his/her way over vision. In this situation, I received permission and blessing from the pastor to run with the vision that he has for the church. He realized how his presence could influence this project. Therefore, he did not attend or add any verbal influence in this project. I infused the research and insight taken from the volunteers so that I could compile a project that will impress a new worship journey for the church.

Some key theological conclusions and rationale that I concluded have been formerly stated in Chapter four, the Literature Review. However, they are worthy of reflection once again in this chapter. One of the theological keys that I stated in Chapter four is that individuals who are responsible for the music in the church must be a theologian. Being a theologian does not mean that one has to have some form of educational competence. It means that there must be a degree of understanding about God.

You cannot influence or lead over an area where you are ignorant. A theologian may feel free to explore other sources about God and potential interest. What we know and believe about God must always be linked with scripture.[193] Scripture inspires us because it is the breath of God according to 2 Timothy 3:16-17. We then worship and lead with intention so that people see and hear God only.

In order to develop greater appreciation for various styles of music as a leader, one must have an honest respect for various forms of artistic expression and the persons doing it. An artist is

---

[193] M. James Sawyer, *The Survivor's Guide to Theology* 1st ed. (Grand Rapids, MI: Zondervan, 2006), 119.

a skilled person who performs. Those who are serving in the area of music in worship must be free to be creative using their gifts and skills.

I have found that artistry does not give birth to true worship; true worship gives birth to artistic expression. I believe that the anointing in worship influences artistic expression. When one gives their gifts to be used in the presence of God, our gifts become bridges to meet people where they are and open them up to becoming more vulnerable to His Divine presence. The nature of God must be seen and realized through artistic expression that penetrates beyond intellect and emotion.[194]

There are a lot of inappropriate songs with bad theologies even though the intent behind the artist's expression may be pure. The primary goal for every artist in worship is to create moments in worship that lead people to becoming more like Jesus. Unchanged lives are visible signs of untrained leaders and possible bad theology. Artistry in worship has the ability to articulate scripture and the message of God in a creative way so that people can be redeemed and be free to express themselves.

Music is one of the most noticeable and common areas of art that has the greatest influence in the church. Therefore, the power that music has when practiced in worship must never be taken lightly.[195] Individuals who operate in that skill and power must operate with responsibility. Artists are communicators, and the creative expressions of that art controls and influences atmosphere.[196] The music that will be shared throughout this project and the focus of this journey will have scriptural influence along with the various experiences of the volunteers.

---

[194] Vernon M. Whaley, *The Role of the Worship Leader Workbook* 2nd ed. (Virginia Beach, VA: Academix, 2012), 57.

[195] Kevin J. Navarro, *The Complete Worship Leader* (Grand Rapids, MI: Baker Books, 2001), 79.

[196] Vernon M. Whaley, *The Role of the Worship Leader Workbook* 2nd ed. (Virginia Beach, VA: Academix, 2012), 69.

This project will also give intentional focus upon how we should glorify God by finding multiple ways to meet the needs of humanity in worship. The volunteers and I will explore multiple genres of music that can be used in worship toward God. God is multifaceted. He can be seen in many ways in this life. I personally believe that he loves multifaceted worship. Worship of our many-faceted God (corporately or privately) should include and embrace many ways of worship.[197] Some of those ways include music, preaching, testifying, artistic expression, etc.

Leaders must recognize that there are many expressions that will suit the needs of the people and the church in worship. In particular for this project, music is the form of expression that is being focus upon. I conclude that music in worship should be multifaceted. Leaders in this space can draw from what is going on in the culture, environment, and the community of the people served and underserved. Clarity and understanding about these will foster productivity and direction.

The styles of music I chose to be presented during this ministry project are: Hymns, Traditional Call and Response, Gospel, and Praise and Worship. All of these styles are common in most churches. However, the issue that surrounds the music currently in most is there is no balance. In Temple #203, which is my chosen ministry setting, the style of music most commonly heard in worship is Traditional Call and Response music and Gospel music. Songs like: "Shine on Me" by Dr. Isaac Watts, "I Will Trust in the Lord" by Rev. C. L Franklin, etc. These are two songs that I have heard them sing in worship services I have attended. They are great songs; however, they isolate a particular generation. They specifically do not connect with Millennials and Post-Millennials.

My thoughts about the previous statement about those songs not connecting with Millennials and Post-Millennials are because both of the songs and writers have greatly contributed to the musical traditions of the historic church. These songs are considered hymns

---

[197] Vernon M. Whaley, *Called to Worship: From the Dawn of Creation to the Final Amen* (Nashville, TN: Thomas Nelson, 2009), 336.

or songs of old. "Hymns are endangered species in this day of praise choruses and video projectors."[198] In this modernized society, culture desires a more contemporary sound. The songs presented above are great songs and should not be thrown away. They are foundational pieces of the Christian faith. The hymns that were sung and written for the church have theological substance which contributed to the spiritual growth of believers. Hymns are useful for prayer, they speak to areas of decision, and they point us toward God.

However, in the Christian Church, the traditional hymns that are commonly sung in the older and traditional churches isolate generations and time periods in the Christian faith. They connect with the struggles of the past rather than the present. The multifaceted God we worship encourages traditional and contemporary music in worship. Whatever style of music, it must be Spirit filled and God focused. There are five participles of diversity in worship that I found in Ephesians. It says, "speaking to one another in psalms and hymns and spiritual songs, singing and making melody in your heart to the Lord," (Eph 5:19). These spirit-filled musical styles edify the church.

Music has the ability to engage individuals in worship. When presenting music in worship, every moment and creative element must be intentional in declaring that God is real and is able to connect with all humanity. It is necessary that leaders be open to different genres of music that possibly could connect at some point in worship with others that may not be part of their generation. An even balance of musical styles presented in worship coupled with the presence of the Holy Spirit is an automatic win in worship.

A few critical things to consider when leading the music:

1. **Music presented in worship must be done in truth and honesty.** Don Wyrtzen said, "truth makes God exclusive."[199] No matter what genre the music is, it must always reveal God. There is power in song and words. Leaders in worship

---

[198] Robert J. Morgan, *Then Sings My Soul Book 2:150 of the World's Greatest Hymn Stories* (Nashville, TN: Thomas Nelson, 2003), xi.

[199] Don Wyrtzen, "Principles of Worship Music and Theology, Part 1." Lecture.

are responsible for the inaccuracies that are communicated in worship. Lyrics must follow theological justifications about God.

2. **Music in worship must make God tangible.** Music has the ability to make God credible in the lives of individuals. In other words, individuals are able to connect when worship is presented in a way that connects with them right where they are. God is the dynamic element of all humanity and our lives are changed as we worship Him.

3. **Music in worship must be balanced.** Freedom, security, and safety are all important principles in worship. Music allows God to be a part of our human experiences. Worship identifies our personal assurance that we have with God. As we worship Him in spirit, the Sprit seals and confirms the bond of love and trust between us, the Father and the incarnate Son.[200]

4. **Music must never be entertainment focused.** Leaders who develop a greater appreciation and understanding for different styles of music must be conscious and careful to never be overtaken by the presentation rather than the presence of the Spirit. Doing that does means losing sight that the music and presentations done during worship should not reflect excellence or lack of skill. The focus of the music must be responsible in "reflecting back the glory of Him who shined down on us, even God, even Christ, even the Holy Ghost."[201]

5. **Difficult music should never be used in congregational worship.** Worship experiences should not be difficult. Jesus made it simple through example. He was a frequent worshipper. A part of His Jewish custom included music and song. In His adolescence, He worshipped and continued as

---

[200] Noel Due, *Created for Worship: From Genesis to Revelation to You* (Scotland: Christian Focus Publications, 2005),17.

[201] A.W. Tozer, *The Purpose of Man* (Ventura, CA: Regal from Gospel Light, 2009), 167.

an adult. During the Last Supper with the disciples, after communion they worshipped and went into a song of praise unto God.

Worship shapes the way we live. When the music presented in worship connects and fulfills its intended purpose, lives are changed. Church of the Living God will have a multi-generational worship gathering that is easy and simple for everyone. It is a two-way street that makes us one with God. We passionately respond to the love of God and the relationship we have developed in our corporate and private journeys.

CHURCH OF THE LIVING GOD WILL HAVE MULTI-GENERATIONAL AND MULTI-CULTURAL GATHERINGS

The key focus of this project is to assist Temple #203 into becoming more culturally intelligent while remaining integral to the scriptures. God yearns for a place to dwell with all humanity. In the Old Testament, He constructed tabernacles as a provision and opportunity to worship with humanity. However, in the New Testament, He desired to remove all boundaries and have a more intimate relationship with all humanity. Instead of having to worship in tabernacles for worship, He desires to dwell in the hearts of men.

That is why we must seek to find a musical style choice that connects God with the hearts of people for multi-generations and multi-cultures. Music is a vehicle that can be used to take the Gospel to the world. It is a universal language that has the ability to cross over many different cultures and generations. As believers, it is our responsibility to point nonbelievers to the Light. The power of this universal language along with the presence of the Holy Spirit makes this happen.

All music does not speak to every culture and generation. Balance and creativity are a necessity when presenting any style of music in worship. Culture is constantly changing, sometimes slowly and gradually, and at other times rapidly and dramatically. Jesus came to save all nations and generations. Every form of religion is flexible based on the cultural mold of man in which it finds itself created.

The foundation of Christianity that has derived from scripture is unshakable.[202] In religion, it is essential that every culture and generation be understood, organized, expressed, and embraced in a manner where Jesus Christ is illumined. Principles must never be watered down to "fit in" with culture.

The influence of culture should never cause the church to lose their salty effectiveness (1 Sam 8 and Matt 5) and give up their call to help reshape and reform culture (John 17).[203] The worship experience will be inclusive for everyone who walks through the doors of that church and there will be an excitement that will spill over into the community. I am convinced that Temple #203 will see unity, growth, and expansion through its new worship format. However, this format cannot be implemented without sufficient assessment and research. The Music Appreciation Course that I created will help facilitate that.

COMPONENTS OF THE MUSIC APPRECIATION COURSE

The Music Appreciation Course created for Temple #203 will expose each attendee to a diversity of music styles coupled with teaching and dialogue in each session. The course will last a minimum of 4 weeks. I will take a portion of the already formatted worship outline of the church and insert it into each session for the sake of consistency and familiarity of the worship culture of Temple #203.

I created a thorough outline that was approved by the International Review Board which looked over and approved my Final Project for this Doctoral Program. The importance of the outline is to help me stay on track each week. This outline will be discussed in more detail in Chapter 6. Every component of this

---

[202] Unknown. *Four Ways Culture Article.*

[203] Ibid.

project has been designed to make clear the roles that need to be played as the ministry moves forward. Listed below are various components of the music appreciation course.

1. I created Pre-and Post-surveys. Each survey will be given to participating volunteers and then given back to me. Each one of them are anonymous and unmarked with no indicators of who filled each one out. Both surveys include musical and spiritual assessment measures. The purpose of these surveys is to provide an awareness and baseline from Week 1 to 4. I will be able to measure if growth, reception, and potential change occurred from the beginning of the course until the end. It will also help me be able to better understand how to facilitate throughout the course what direction, different avenues, and innovations will be useful for enhancing worship in the life of Temple #203.

2. Each session will be a maximum of 90 minutes. Each session will be presented to a small group of 8-15 volunteers weekly. These sessions are so compact that it could easily take up to ten weeks to cover everything. However, four weeks is the maximum amount of time that I was allowed to schedule on the church calendar.

3. Each session will be opened with the same format but have different styles of music inserted in the worship format that are familiar as well as foreign to the music culture of the church.

Week 1 – Traditional Devotional Music. All religions have their own style of devotional songs. One of the musical styles that is often used in worship by the ministry setting includes devotional songs. These songs are spirited call-and-response songs of testimony and personal reflection that give glory to God. These songs have been handed down from one generation to the next. Many mainline denominations like the Presbyterian, Methodist, Baptist, and Catholic churches use a more traditional influence and style of music in worship. This kind of music is not really picturesque in the modern and emerging church currently. However, the culture of this church cannot get rid of traditional music.

Week 2 – Contemporary Praise and Worship Music. This musical style is relatively the music of our time now. It is the popular music in the church that is driven from what is heard more on radio and pushed through popular culture. This type of music is typically the musical choice for younger generations. There are many styles to this genre. In most situations, contemporary music has evolved from choirs to ensembles and included some signature instruments in the church to a more modern and concert feel. This music encourages congregational participation with focus on adoration toward God.

Week 3 – Traditional Hymns. This style of music encourages congregational participation as well. However, this music historically does not attract many younger generations because the music is not their preference. This musical style generally attracts and ministers to a more elderly generation.

Week 4 – Blended Music. This music is a mixture of traditional, contemporary, historic, and experiential music. This style is not always successful because knowing what to keep and what to let go can be challenging. Therefore, when trying to find the right style choice that will close the gap between the elderly and the youth, it must be intentionally focused and properly prepared. This style of music mixes instrumentation, hymns, praise and worship, and seeks to touch every generation for all humanity.

THE PRIMARY AUDIENCE

The primary audience for this project is a small, diverse group of individuals. Many churches suffer from small groups. Small groups have the ability to reduce the efficiency of the overall operation, reduce morale, and may contribute to the demise of a productive company culture.[204] This is why it is essential that the group reflects diversity. A diverse group that will include different ages, areas of ministry in which they serve in the church, and multi-cultures, etc.

This approach can be risky because conflict and argument are possible in the midst of discussion. As the only project leader for this project, I have to have control the temperament in each session. Everyone who is present in each session is a volunteer and is on the same level with the other volunteers. Each session will carry an environment of unity, commonality, community, collaboration, and integration of the information that will be collected in each session. Every voice will be heard. You cannot promote change without knowing what needs have to be met. By the end of four weeks, we will be able to provide a solution to the needs and purpose of this project.

Each session will include the same formatted worship flow until the final week. That format will include the Lord's Prayer, Scripture (Psalm 100), and a 2-song worship set facilitated each week by different volunteers. The final session will include a simulated worship service that will be formatted in the third week session. It will include the musical style that was found to be the best suited for this ministry setting. Each section in this chapter provided a snapshot and projection for what will take place during this final project. The next chapter is an actual view of how each session will be carried during this final project.

---

[204] "Online Business Dictionary - BusinessDictionary.com." Online Business Dictionary - BusinessDictionary.com. Accessed August 11, 2019 from http://www. businessdictionary.com/.

CHAPTER SIX

Ministry Project Implementation and Evaluation

MUSIC AND WORSHIP SEMINAR

There was a lot of hard work put into the preparation and implementation of this project. This chapter examines this project from the beginning to the end. I began working on this project around July 2017. I started with some initial research on my proposed topic of interest. In my research, I had to see if there were any other individuals who had already done this topic. I did find many similar dissertations and thesis on this topic. However, there weren't many projects done on this particular topic nor anything specific on what I believed to be the prescription for a struggling church. They were mostly assessments rather than what I believe my project is, an antidote.

I further began to seek relative resources that would aid in the integrity of this project. After exhaustive research, I did some minor things that helped to infuse my hunger and passion for the development and creation of my final project. I began building my Bibliography. After that, one of my classes had me do my first draft of Chapter three, which is on my Theology of Community and Ministry. After I completed some exhaustive research and those drafts, I left the project alone until around July 2018. My focus until then was on my classes in the Doctoral of Ministry program. Around July 2018 is when I began to start working aggressively on this project again. The projected time for implementation was October 2018 after the initial process of approval was done from the Program Director and Review Board for this project.

The seminar for this project was set to begin on the first Saturday in October. There was no time to waste. This was the only available time the ministry setting had available to do my project. Therefore, I had to work diligently every day and sometimes over 30-hours a week preparing for this project. The premises of this project were set to have a minimum of 8-10 volunteers between the ages 18 – 64. The actual median age of the volunteers that attended each session for this project that I gauged were between their 40s – 70s. This is reflective of the median age at Temple #203, also referred to as the ministry setting, which is around 50s. Any larger number of volunteers would hinder the ability of the project group in having a more intimate and productive weekly sessions within the short timeframe allotted to complete the project. A lot had to be covered in four weeks and every voice was important for this project.

The different ages needed for this project will contribute diverse insights and generational points of view that helped in my research. I would have personally liked to have had some volunteers in their 20s and 30s to provide a more youthful perspective. However, that age demographic does not have sizeable presence in Temple #203. The lack of that present age group did not stop me from receiving valuable and tangible insight from the ages represented. Each volunteer was passionate about how they independently chose to worship as well as the type of music they desire while in worship.

This small group setting was intentionally designed to be small and intimate so that true and honest discussions would take place. In order for that to occur, I intentionally created a synergy each week where the attitudes, mood, and choices we made in our discussions were healthy and mutually reinforcing for the goals of the project. I also used some of Peter Steinke's health promoters for small group discussions. Those promoters were, "purpose, appraisal and management of conflict, clarity, mood and tone, mature interaction, healing capacities, and a focus on resources."[205] My goal each week was to make sure that we did not get stuck on issues and weaknesses of the ministry setting. We remained focused on strength, options, and resources so that we could build morale and expectations to meet the outlined goals of this project.

When there are diverse mindsets, conflict is inevitable, and disagreements will take place. Also, power play in conflict can become an issue too. Some of the volunteers are not a part of the Music Ministry where this project would directly affect them. The ones who serve in the Music Ministry were more passionate and defensive about the issues that directly involve the music ministry. Other power play could have come from the older volunteers. They had greater influence over all things in the church because of their "seniority."

Highly anxious parties can easily become defensive and then the group could fall into a spiral of opposition.[206] I had to constantly be sensitive to the emotional system of the group so that no threat of hostility had begun to take place. During those times when the group began to feel tense and anxious, I had steered the group back into focus. It was important that the environment remained safe so that everyone's voice was respected.

Bernard Mayer said that there are six broad needs that people want in groups especially when conflict emerges. Those needs are *voice, validation, vindication, procedural justice, impact, and safety.*[207] The *voice* is the most fundamental need. Everyone wants to be heard

---

[205] Peter L. Steinke, *Healthy Congregations* (Lanham, MD: Rowman & Littlefield, 2006), 28.

[206] Ibid., 54.

[207] Bernard Mayer, *The Dynamics of Conflict Resolution* (San Francisco, CA: Jossey-Bass, 2000), Chapter 6.

by those who matter to them. Every volunteer at each session mattered because they all shared the same interest in the topic presented each week. Therefore, it was my responsibility to make sure that the focus was upon everyone understanding each other.

Each session more and more things were uncovered about the corporate worship. Some of them included the following: the length of service, selection of music, and even lack of preparation from the Music Ministry. The issues shared did not stop me from remaining focused on the direction and vision for the project, so that each session would influence excitement, increase, and quality involvement each session.

As I communicated in each session, I was precise, with no misleading communication, or vague statements that left doors open for varying interpretations. A very detailed outline was needed for this project. When discussing a topic like this, it can be intense and emotional, open doors for misunderstanding because of misinterpretation. If I did not have the answer to any question or a ready response to anyone, I would ask if I could follow back up with them the next session. When the waters are troubled and increased hostility is present, pursuing avenues of peace makes the difference.[208] Therefore, my words had to be carefully chosen. Misunderstandings were not beneficial in the midst of a passionate group with a topic that is divisive.

RESOURCES NEEDED

The resources needed for this project were minimal. I did not need a lot of materials, staff, or stock of supplies for this project. Most of the work has been done through research and interviews Additional work was completed through the sessions in this project. The flyer was created on my personal computer and approved by the Project Director who was overseeing and mentoring me through the creation of this Final Project. After it was approved,

---

[208] Kenneth Sande, *The Peacemaker* (Grand Rapids, MI: Baker Books, 2004), 176.

I emailed it to the Church Administrator for print. This flyer was used for announcements during worship for a couple of weeks and then to be placed at the information table where all the other upcoming events were.

The next set of forms that needed to be printed were the self-consent forms. These forms were essential for each volunteer to sign at the beginning of the first week session. This form was designed to get consent from each volunteer of their participation in this project. I also created two different surveys and a brief outline of the seminar to be printed. Temple #203 was gracious to make the copies for the attendees at no cost to me and this project. All of these items were completed a few weeks before the project began.

The dates for the Seminar were four Saturdays, October 6, 13, 20, 27, 2018 from 12:00pm – 1:30pm. Each session was held on site in the sanctuary. A deacon of the church opened the doors for us weekly. In the sanctuary, I was given access to musical instruments (keyboard, organ, drums), audio (three handheld microphones), the podium, and extension cord for my computer. The only other resource needed were the presence of the volunteers.

PRE-SURVEY

For the first session of the seminar, there were a lot of different components involved. Several items had to be addressed before going into the session. Because I expected for this to be a small group, I did all of the leg work myself. Each volunteer upon entry of the sanctuary was asked to sign a self-consent form and then a pre-survey. The purpose of the pre-survey was to ask each volunteer to share their honest thoughts about the worship at Temple #203 and in their personal life. Below are some of the results from the pre-survey.

TABLE 6.1 RESULTS FOR PRE-SURVEY

GENDER M/F	AGE	YEARS ATTENDED COTLG #203	CURRENT SATISFACTION	STYLE CHOICE OF MUSIC
FEMALE - 12	19 – 35: 1	1-3 YEARS: 1	VERY SATISFIED: 8	TRADITIONAL: 2
MALE - 2	50-64: 9	3-10 YEARS: 2	SOMEWHAT SATISFIED: 3	CONTEMPORARY: 2
	65+: 2	OVER 10 YEARS: 8		BLENDED: 7

PREFERED MUSIC IN CORPORATE WORSHIP	PREFERRED MUSIC IN INDIVIDUAL WORSHIP	AREAS OF IMPORTANCE: TOP 3 (TIME, SERMON, WORSHIP PARTICIPATION, TYPE OF MUSIC, FELLOWSHIP)
CONTEMPORARY (PRAISE & WORSHIP): 11	CONTEMPORARY (PRAISE & WORSHIP): 10	WORSHIP PARTICIPATION: 3
TRADITIONAL(HYMNS): 11	TRADITIONAL(HYMNS): 11	SERMON: 5
OTHER: 2	OTHER:	TIME: 3

OUTLINE OF PROJECT

After completion of all of the consent and pre-survey forms, it was time to begin the session. Below is a summarized outline of the Master Outline used weekly during the project. In the Appendix is the actual Master Outline. As the leader and teacher during the project, it was important that I was fully prepared. In order to be productive, preparation was essential so that the group would remain focused and so the set goals for each week would be accomplished. The volunteers had a more concise version of the outline. However, for the purpose of clarity of what was exactly taught and discussed in each session; I am providing my exhausted version. A good portion of what was taught in each session is consistent with what is found in each chapter.

WEEK 1

SURVEY
- Pass out Pre-Survey and give a minimum of 10 minutes to for attendees to complete.

WORSHIP FORMAT

PRAYER

SCRIPTURE

2 SONG WORSHIP SET – *(VIDEO PRESENTATION OF WORSHIP OR HAVE A DIFFERENT WORSHIP LEADER EACH WEEK – DIVERSE LEADERS)*

REFLECTION
- 15-minute discussion and analyzation about the worship just presented.

PURPOSE AND GOALS FOR THIS PROJECT

This course will last for a minimum of four sessions. This course will expose attendees to a diversity of styles and advocates of those styles which are designed to also be worshipful. The intent is to show that change and unity was promoted, possible, and fruitful in this otherwise potentially divisive area of worship music. The conclusive intent from this project is to facilitate greater harmony between evolving generations in worship experiences and to make the worship at the Church of the Living God an inclusive experience.

THE EVOLUTION OF WORSHIP IN A MINISTRY SETTING
- Identify ministry needs to make worship more inclusive.

THEOLOGY OF BIBLICAL WORSHIP
- Biblical Influences
- Cultural Influences
- Biblical Language of Worship

QUESTIONS

WEEK 2

WORSHIP FORMAT

PRAYER

SCRIPTURE

2 SONG WORSHIP SET – *(VIDEO PRESENTATION*
OF WORSHIP OR HAVE A DIFFERENT WORSHIP
LEADER EACH WEEK – DIVERSE LEADERS)

REFLECTION

- **15 MINUTE DISCUSSION AND ANALYZATION ABOUT THE WORSHIP FORMAT FOR THE WEEK PRESENTED**

ANCIENT – FUTURE WORSHIP

- Traditional vs. Contemporary Worship Models

MUSIC INFLUENCES IN THE CHURCH

- Sacred Music Influences
- Secular Music Influences

MISSING GENERATIONS IN THE CHURCH

- The ages from 18 – 35 years old are coming up missing in the church because the culture in our communities and in the world has shifted. The youth that are in the churches now are those who more than likely grew up in the church. The ones that have not grew up in church are saying that church doesn't fit them. A greater percentage of those between the ages mentioned above are deciding not to come back into church for several reasons that include the issue of worship. Leadership is not embracing the needs of this generation. The worship services are simply repeating itself in churches without embracing change or being open minded to rethink how they do church in this age to win the lost generations.

QUESTIONS

WEEK 3

WORSHIP FORMAT

PRAYER

SCRIPTURE

2 SONG WORSHIP SET – *(VIDEO PRESENTATION OF WORSHIP OR HAVE A DIFFERENT WORSHIP LEADER EACH WEEK – DIVERSE LEADERS)*

REFLECTION
- **15 MINUTE DISCUSSION AND ANALYZATION ABOUT THE WORSHIP FORMAT FOR THE WEEK PRESENTED**

DEMOGRAPHIC SURVEY
- Church Community
- Unchurch Community

PURPOSE OF A CULTURALLY INFLUENCED WORSHIP
- Greater harmony and unity amongst the membership as it learns to appreciate the diverse ways we worship individually and corporately.

BENEFITS OF CREATING AN INCLUSIVE AND CULTURALLY SENSITIVE WORSHIP FORMAT

- Personal Benefit
- Corporate Benefit

QUESTIONS

WEEK 4

WORSHIP FORMAT

PRAYER
SCRIPTURE
2 SONG WORSHIP SET – *(VIDEO PRESENTATION
OF WORSHIP OR HAVE A DIFFERENT WORSHIP
LEADER EACH WEEK – DIVERSE LEADERS)*

REFLECTION

- **15 MINUTE DISCUSSION AND ANALYZATION ABOUT THE WORSHIP FORMAT FOR THE WEEK PRESENTED**

INNOVATIONS IN WORSHIP

- *There needs to be some new innovations to their worship services to draw the absent generations in the church*:
    1. Our motivation to see those generations worshipping God.
    2. The worship will become more missional which is living out the Gospel.
    3. It will address both cultural and generational change.
    4. Shows good stewardship of the finances and building the kingdom of God.
    5. It sparks relationships and keeps the church from dying out.
- Innovations in worship ideas

CREATING AN INCLUSIVE WORSHIP FORMAT

- Group participation

POST SURVEY

POST-SURVEY

A post-survey was given to each attendee. Every attendee that started at the beginning of the Seminar did not make it to the final session. However, I had enough there to help me measure the productivity of the Seminar. This survey is a little different from the post. It should be able to help me measure growth, change in mindset, and if the project fulfilled its purpose. There were many interesting findings that will be further discussed.

TABLE 6.2 RESULTS FOR POST-SURVEY

CURRENT SATISFACION	STYLE CHOICE OF MUSIC	PREFERED MUSIC IN CORPORATE WORSHIP
VERY SATISFIED: 3	TRADITIONAL: 2	CONTEMPORARY (PRAISE & WORSHIP): 9
SOMEWHAT SATISFIED: 5	CONTEMPORARY: 1	TRADITIONAL(HYMNS): 8
NEITHER: 1	BLENDED: 6	OTHER:

PREFERRED MUSIC IN INDIVIDUAL WORSHIP	OPEN TO NEW EXPRESSIONS IN WORSHIP	WHICH STYLE ENGAGED W MORE IN SESSION
CONTEMPORARY (PRAISE & WORSHIP): 8	YES: 8	TRADITIONAL: 3
TRADITIONAL(HYMNS): 4	NO:	CONTEMPORARY: 9
OTHER:		

DISCOVERIES MADE

There were a lot of discoveries made during each session. When integrating worship into the life and vision of the church, I found different integrated silos in the church. There were several representations of ministries and dynamics in the church at each session. Everyone present was not just from the Music Ministry. The mindset of the majority saw worship as an individual component separated from the other church ministries.

The problem with this mindset is it causes integration and a wedge between the other ministries of the church. Some of the discussions isolated the Music Ministry and there was a sense of division and acceptance of the way things are because of the issues in the Music Ministry. When there is an "us and them" mentality, it makes it difficult to unify what is needed in worship. That was an issue that I had to spend some time addressing and educating the group.

I presented a unified goal for each session. The atmosphere was staged that we all were working together to meet that goal. This created a natural connection and synergy with each individual and ministry represented. Worship is a passionate issue, therefore negotiating was going to take place and that had to be understood with the group. I communicated to the group that we are a body, not a business. Every organism has to share space and work its area to fulfill the same goal. Each week we collaborated together to meet the goal of this final project. Further discoveries that I found during each session were:

1. The majority of the attendees were Very Satisfied with the music and current format of worship at Temple #203. This is interesting because the discussions we had weekly showed the opposite of what was the actual feeling about the music and current worship format of the church. Only 3 volunteers shared on their surveys that they were Somewhat Satisfied. I concluded that there should have been a larger number for Somewhat Satisfied or Dissatisfied.

2. The majority of the volunteers desired a more blended style of worship which included traditional hymns, call and response, choirs, praise and worship, organs, drums, etc. I stayed with the majority style choice of music and implemented it into my project goals.

3. The 3 areas that had the highest numbers in level of importance from the surveys were the Sermon, Worship Participation, and Time. As I stated above, the area in

worship that had the highest number of importance in worship was the Sermon. The interesting factor of this is the area of Music was not a part of the top 3. As discussion continued, I realize that was because there is a lack of confidence in the productivity of the Music Ministry.

4. At the final session, a post-survey was given. The number of volunteers who were Very Satisfied with the music and current worship format at the first session decreased. That was what I expected. The number of volunteers who marked that they were Somewhat Satisfied increased. This change showed me that there were some mindset changes from the beginning of the seminar and that individuals were being enlightened about what is actually needed.

SUGGESTIONS FOR IMPLEMENTATION

The building block to growth and development is education and learning. Anything that does not grow or being maintained properly is subject to failure and breakdown. After exhaustive research it is clear that people have different ideas about worship.[209] Each intimate session with the volunteers showed me diversity, however a unified mindset that they care about how worship is done individually and corporately.

Each session was structured intentionally for growth and education. Each week we did simulated worships that were effective for discussion and setting the tone spiritually for each session. The opening worship sets never changed, just the music. This showed that different styles of music have the ability to also be effective in an already structured format of worship. The only analysis I would make with using the same format is that it did not build or prepare completely for the new format that was presented in the final week. However, we did discuss the things that could be beneficial and the ones that could be taken out in their current worship format.

---

[209] Greg Scheer, *The Art of Worship: A Musician's Guide to Leading Modern Worship* (Grand Rapids, MI: Baker Books, 2006), 16.

According to the presurvey and earlier discussions, the majority of the volunteers stated that the most important thing in worship to them was the sermon. With that in mind, I considered presenting a Thematic Worship Structure. This kind of structure is sermon-dominated and everything that takes place before and after centers around the message. However, this structure isolated the sermon as a separate component of worship. The passion from the volunteers concerning that mindset almost caused me to change my course. If this began to influence me, I know how it easily influences the entire ministry at large. Therefore, I backed off of that type of structure. I believe that the sermon should be considered as a part of worship rather than a separate component in worship. There was a day when preaching built churches numerically. However, that day has changed. That mindset must do the same.

Each session allowed each volunteer to be individual concerning what they felt was important and beneficial so that worship could be more inclusive and successful for all generations. Gravitating to a particular mindset would have made this project ineffective and non-essential. My responsibility during this project was not to conform to the original mindset. As the leader of this project it was to guide us on a journey to build what would work for this particular ministry setting and community to build an effective worship format. At times that would mean that I had to challenge the group in areas that may have been uncomfortable and difficult to embrace. I also had to be sure that any projected changes prescribed were given only after proper assessment was done. The answers and prescription given had to make sense and had to be tangible to promote immediate changes.

I decided to approach presenting to them an Experiential Service Structure. This type of service is emotional, music driven, and structured around getting a response from the worshippers. This type of worship would work well for the Ancient-Future style of worship that I have presented to the volunteers for their corporate worship format. Some things that needed to be kept in mind as we moved toward an actual implementation model for the church. We had to develop a philosophy that included wisdom, resources of age, and an understanding of scripture for all generations. Otherwise the current ministry setting would be vulnerable to losing their identity, adapt to consumerism, have continued division in the body, and will be waring between reverence and relevance in worship.

In the last session, we simulated a new worship structure that included a blended style of music. The only challenge I had with this is I did not have the support of every entity that would be considered the worship team. Although, music was the major focus, it is essential that every leader and team where this new format would impact needed to be a part of this project. Those individuals included the ministers, media, musicians, greeters, ushers, etc. With that being said, I would have also needed more than four weeks to do this project. This could have lasted easily up to eight weeks. That would have given me more time to deal with each individual ministry as all the dots were connected for the upcoming changes.

Therefore, I was only able to measure the individual responses rather than a corporate response at the completion of this project. Those individual responses were highlighted in the Post Surveys found in Table 8. At the beginning of this project, I knew that it was going to be a journey that would have to be continued. I am proud and satisfied with what was accomplished.

It is easy to conclude that one person cannot make a difference. However, I believe that when one is mastered by the message, they have the power to influence others in that same direction.[210]

I submitted the new worship format to the pastor. That was the furthest I was able to take this project at this time; however, my desire is to see this all the way through. I plan on doing some follow up with the him and with any of his leaders if allowed to so that we can see what more can be done to assist in their journey of worship. The intention of this project was not to walk them hand-in-hand from start to finish initially, but to deposit seeds that will hopefully be watered over a period of time.

---

[210] Kevin J. Navarro, *The Complete Worship Leader* (Grand Rapids, MI: Baker Books, 2001), 53.

The church needed tangible changes in the music and worship so that they will experience measurable growth. Growth without change and evolution is impossible to manifest. It is reflective of what takes place in our individual bodies on the inside and outside. However, if intentional care done to the inside of the body is not done as much as it is to the outward appearance of our bodies. The body will suffer and fade away. It is the inward things that causes the body to fall apart and even die. This project was an intentional prognosis for an aging and suffering church to find tangible ways to be restored back to being a flourishing church that will reflect back the glory of Him who shined down on us, even God, even Christ, even the Holy Ghost.[211] I am confident that the research efforts and information given in each chapter that helped to assert the needed changes for this church will significantly impact this local church and even the universal church at large in a positively.

---

[211] A.W. Tozer, *The Purpose of Man* (Ventura, CA: Regal from Gospel Light, 2009), 167.

BIBLIOGRAPHY

Best, Harold M. *Unceasing Worship: Biblical Perspectives on Worship and the Arts.* Downers Grove, IL: InterVarsity Press, 2003.

Bird, Warren, Ed Stetzer, and Elmer Towns. *11 Innovations in the Local Church.* Ventura, CA: Regal Books, 2007.

Black, Kathy. *Culturally-Conscious Worship.* St. Louis, MO: Chalice Press, 2000.

Bradley, C. Randall. *From Postlude to Prelude: Music Ministry's Other Six Days* Fenton, MO: Morning Star Music Publishers, 2004.

Brooks, Steven D. *Worship Quest: An Exploration of Worship Leadership.* Eugene, OR: Wipf and Stock, 2015.

Bullock, C. Hassell. *Encountering the Book of Psalms (encountering Biblical Studies) a Literary and Theological Introduction.* Grand Rapids, MI: Baker Academic, 2004.

Christianity Today, "Leadership Surveys Church Conflict." 2004.

Davis, John J. *Worship and the Reality of God: An Evangelical Theology of Real Presence.* Downers Grove, IL: InterVarsity Press, 2010.

Donne, John. "XVII. Meditation." In *Devotions upon Emergent Occasions.*

Erickson, Millard J. *Christian Theology.* Grand Rapids, MI: Baker Academic, 2013.

Farhadian, Charles E. *Christian Worship Worldwide: Expanding Horizons, Deepening Practices.* Grand Rapids, MI: Eerdmans, 2007.

Foster, Charles. *The Story of the Bible from Genesis to Revelation Told in Simple Language.* Philadelphia, PA: Charles Foster, 1873.

Henry, Matthew and Church, Leslie. *Commentary on the whole Bible: Genesis to Revelation* – Grand Rapids, MI: Zondervan, 1961.

Hill, A. E. *Enter His Courts with Praise!: Old Testament Worship for the New Testament Church.* Grand Rapids, MI: Baker, 1993.

House, Brad. *Community: Taking Your Small Group Off Life Support.* Wheaton, IL: Crossway 2011.

Icenogle, Gareth Weldon. *Biblical Foundations for Small Group Ministry: An Integrational Approach.* Downers Grove, IL: IVP, 1994.

Kauflin, Bob. *Worship Matters: Leading Others to Encounter with Greatness of God.* Wheaton, IL: Crossway Books, 2008.

Kimball, Dan. *Emerging Worship: Creating Worship Gatherings for New Generations.* Grand Rapids, MI: Zondervan, 2004.

Krabill, James R., Frank Fortunato, Robin P. Harris, and Brian Schrag. *Worship and the Mission for the Global Church: An Ethnodoxology Handbook.* Pasadena, CA: William Carrey Library, 2012.

Man, Ron. *Proclamation and Praise: Hebrews 2:12 and the Christology of Worship.* Eugene, OR: Wipf & Stock Publishers, 2007.

Mathena, Gary M. *One Thing Needful: An Invitation to the Study of Worship.* Bloomington, IN: CrossBooks., 2013.

Maxwell, John C. *The 360 Leader: Developing Your Influence from Anywhere in the Organization.* Nashville, TN: Thomas Nelson, 2011.

Mayer, Bernard S. *The Dynamics of Conflict: A Guide to Engagement and Intervention.* San Francisco, CA: Jossey-Bass, 2012.

McBeth, H. Leon. *Baptist Heritage: Four Centuries of Baptist Witness.* Nashville, TN: Broadman and Holman, 2016.

McFague, Sallie. *Life Abundant: Rethinking Theology and Economy for a Planet in Peril.* Minneapolis, MN: Fortress Press, 2001.

McIntosh, Gary L. and Rima, Samuel D. *Overcoming the Dark Side of Leadership: How to Become an Effective Leader by Confronting Potential Failures.* Grand Rapids, MI: Baker Books, 2007.

McNeal, Reggie. *Present Future: Six Tough Questions for the Church.* Hoboken, NJ: John Wiley & Sons, 2003.

McRaney, Jr Will. *Unceasing Worship: The Art of Personal Evangelism.* Nashville, TN: B & H Publishing Group, 2003.

Meyers, Ruth A. *Missional Worship, Worshipful Mission: Gathering as God's People, Going Out....* Grand Rapids, MI: Eerdmans, 2014.

Morgenthaler, Sally. *Worship Evangelism: Inviting Unbelievers into the Presence of God.* Grand Rapids, MI: Zondervan, 1999.

Niebuhr, H. Richard. *Christ and Culture.* New York: Harper & Row, 1975.

Noland, Rory. *Worship on Earth as it is in Heaven: Exploring Worship as a Spiritual Discipline.* Grand Rapids, MI: Zondervan, 2011.

Official manual with the doctrines and discipline of the Church of God in Christ, 1973. Memphis, TN: Church of God in Christ, Pub. Board, 1991.

Paris, Jenell Williams, and Brian M. Howell. *Introducing Cultural Anthropology: A Christian Perspective.* Grand Rapids, MI: Baker Academic, 2010.

Peterson, David G. *Engaging with God: A Biblical Theology of Worship.* Downers Grove, IL: InterVarsity Press, 1992.

Pinson, J. Matthew. *Perspectives on Christian Worship: Five Views.* Nashville, TN: Broadman and Holman, 2009.

Price, III, Timothy. *Music Appreciation Course.* Fairview Heights, IL, 2018.

Rah, Soong Chan. *Many Colors: Cultural Intelligence for a Changing Church.* Chicago: Moody Publishers, 2010.

Redman, Robb. *The Great Worship Awakening: Singing a New Song in the Postmodern Church.* San Francisco, CA: Jossey-Bass, 2002.

Redman, Matt. *The Heart of Worship Files.* Minnesota, MN: Bethany House, 2003.

Rhodes, Ron. *The Complete Guide to Christian Denominations.* Eugene, OR: Harvest House Publishers, 2015.

Ross, Allen P. *Recalling the Hope of Glory: Biblical Worship from the Garden to the New Creation.* Grand Rapids, MI: Kregel Publications, 2006.

Sawyer, M. James. *The Survivor's Guide to Theology*. Grand Rapids, MI: Zondervan, 2006.

Scheer, Greg. *The Art of Worship: A Musician's Guide to Leading Modern Worship*. Grand Rapid, MI: Baker Books, 2006.

Schilder, Klass. *Christ and Culture*. Winnipeg: Premier, 1977.

Steinke, Peter L. *Healthy Congregations*. Lanham, MD: Rowman & Littlefield Publishers, 2006.

Stetzer, Ed and Thom S. Rainer. *Transformational Church*. Nashville, TN: B&H Publishing, 2010.

The Doctrines and Discipline of the African Methodist Episcopal Church. Chapel Hill, NC: University of North Carolina at Chapel Hill Library, 2017.

Torrance, James. *Worship, Community, and the Triune God of Grace*. Downers Grove, IL: InterVarsity Press, 1996.

Townley, Cathy. *Missional Worship: Increasing Attendance and Expanding the Boundaries of Your Church*. St. Louis, MO: Chalice Press, 2011.

Towns, Elmer, and Edward Stetzer. *Perimeters of Light: Biblical Boundaries for the Emerging Church*. Chicago: Moody Publishers, 2004.

Towns, Elmer L. and Whaley, Vernon M. *Worship Through the Ages: How the Great Awakenings Shape Evangelical Worship*. Nashville, TN: B & H Publishing, 2012.

Tozer, A.W. *The Purpose of Man*. Ventura, CA: Regal from Gospel Light, 2009.

Tylor, Edward B. *Primitive Culture: Researches into the Development of Mythology, Philosophy, Religion, Art, and Custom.* London: John Murray, 1871.

Van Gelder, Craig. *Confident Witness—Changing World: Rediscovering the Gospel in North America.* Grand Rapids, MI: Wm. B. Eerdmans, 1999.

_____. *The Essence of the Church: A Community Created by the Spirit.* Grand Rapids, MI: Baker, 2000.

_____. "From Corporate Church to Missional Church: The Challenge Facing Congregations Today." *Review and Expositor* 101, no. 3 (2004): 425-46.

_____. *The Missional Church in Context: Helping Congregations Develop Contextual Ministry.* Grand Rapids, MI: Wm. B. Eerdmans, 2007.

_____. *The Ministry of the Missional Church: A Community Led by the Spirit.* Grand Rapids, MI: Baker, 2007.

_____. *The Missional Church and Leadership Formation: Helping Congregations Develop Leadership Capacity.* Grand Rapids, MI: Wm. B. Eerdmans, 2009.

Van Gelder, Craig, and Dwight J. Zscheile. *The Missional Church in Perspective: Mapping Trends and Shaping the Conversation.* Grand Rapids, MI: Baker Academic, 2011.

Walters, Michael. *Can't Wait for Sunday: Leading Your Congregation in Authentic Worship.* Indianapolis, IN: Wesleyan Publishing House, 2006.

Webber, Robert E. *Worship Old and New.* Grand Rapids, MI: Zondervan Publishing House, 1994.

Whaley, Vernon M. *WRSP 502 History and Philosophy of Worship Workbook*. 2nd ed. Virginia Beach, VA: Academx, 2013.

_____. *The Dynamics of Corporate Worship*. 2nd ed. Virginia Beach, VA: Academx, 2009.

_____. *Called to Worship: From the Dawn of Creation to the Final Amen*. Nashville, TN: Thomas Nelson, 2009.

Wheeler, David and Whaley, Vernon. *The Great Commission to Worship: Biblical Principles for Worship-Based Evangelism*. Nashville, TN: B & H Publishing Group, 2011.

_____. *Worship and Witness: Becoming a Great Commission Worshiper*. Nashville, TN: LifeWay Press, 2012.

Willmington, Matt. "Silos in Ministry." *Liberty University*, 2016.

Invitation to Participate

Invitation to Participate
Music and Worship Appreciation

INVITATION TO PARTICIPATE IN A
4 WEEK COURSE
THE NEXT LEVEL OF WORSHIP
CONDUCTED BY,
ELD. TIMOTHY PRICE, III
For more information: afterthis314@gmail.com
Ages 18 – 64 are welcome

Appendix B

Music Worship Appreciation Pre-Survey

2018 MUSIC WORSHIP APPRECIATION PRE-SURVEY

Please help us compile research as we facilitate avenues and innovations to better understand and enhance the worship life of the church! Please take a few moments to answer these questions and then return the survey ASAP. We invite EVERY PERSON who is taking this survey to attend the Music and Worship Appreciation Course. Dates will be announced.

1. Name and area of ministry serve in at church?

    _____

2. What is your gender?
    - ☐ Male
    - ☐ Female

3. How old are you?
    - ☐ 12-18
    - ☐ 19-35
    - ☐ 36-49
    - ☐ 50-64
    - ☐ 65+

4. How long have you attended worship at the Church of the Living God?
    - ☐ Less than one year
    - ☐ 1-3 years
    - ☐ 3-10 years
    - ☐ Over 10 years

5. How often do you typically attend worship at the Church of the Living God?
   - ❏ Every week
   - ❏ 2-3 times each month
   - ❏ Once a month
   - ❏ Only on holidays
   - ❏ Sporadically
   - ❏ Other (ex. Holidays, Funerals, Weddings)_____
   _____

6. Do you have children living at home? YES NO
   - ❏ If so, do they typically attend worship with you? YES NO
   - ❏ What are their ages? _____

7. Which worship service do you primarily attend?
   - ❏ Sunday at 10:15am
   - ❏ Wednesday at 6:45pm

8. What is your CURRENT SATISFACTION with the worship service you primarily attend?
   - ❏ Very Satisfied
   - ❏ Somewhat Satisfied
   - ❏ Neither Satisfied or Dissatisfied
   - ❏ Somewhat Dissatisfied
   - ❏ Very Dissatisfied

9. Which worship style do you MOST prefer?
   - ❏ Traditional – Choir, Hymnals, use of the organ, use of liturgy such as responsive reading, creeds and Lord's Prayer
   - ❏ Contemporary – Music on screen only, mostly praise music, use of guitar/drums, minimal use of liturgy.
   - ❏ Blended – A mixture of both traditional and contemporary styles.
   - ❏ Other _____

10. Which style of music do you MOST prefer in Corporate Worship at Shalom? (You may pick up to 2)
    - ☐ Hymns
    - ☐ Contemporary Gospel
    - ☐ Traditional Gospel
    - ☐ Christian Rap
    - ☐ Christian Rock
    - ☐ Praise and Worship
    - ☐ None

11. Which style of music do you MOST prefer in your Private Worship time? (You may pick up to 2)
    - ☐ Hymns
    - ☐ Contemporary Gospel
    - ☐ Traditional Gospel
    - ☐ Christian Rap
    - ☐ Christian Rock
    - ☐ Praise and Worship
    - ☐ None

12. What is your CURRENT SATISFACTION with the start time of the service you primarily attend?
    - ☐ Very Satisfied
    - ☐ Somewhat Satisfied
    - ☐ Neither Satisfied or Dissatisfied
    - ☐ Somewhat Dissatisfied
    - ☐ Very Dissatisfied

13. Rank order from 1 to 5 how important each of these factors are in choosing which worship service you would primarily attend (1 is the most important, 5 is the least important)?
    - ____ What time the service starts
    - ____ Type of Music
    - ____ The Sermon
    - ____ When I participate in worship (Choir, Liturgist, etc.)
    - ____ My friend/family attend the same service

14. Please rate how much you agree or disagree with the following statements:

	Strongly Agree	Agree	Neutral	Disagree	Strongly Disagree
The music during the worship service is a main component of how I express my spiritual joy.					
I would be interested in worshipping in a space other than the sanctuary.					
I often receive a sense of God's presence during congregational worship.					
I am often bored during worship services and anxious to have it over.					
I attend worship services only because I feel it is my duty.					
Availability of childcare is an important factor in whether or not I can attend worship or Sunday School programs.					

15. Would you be willing to participate in a 4-week Music and Worship Appreciation Course?
    ☐ Yes
    ☐ No

Are they any comments you would like to make?

Appendix C

Music Worship Appreciation Post-Survey

2018 MUSIC WORSHIP APPRECIATION COURSE POST-SURVEY

As we prepare to conclude the course of our research. Please help us compile post research information to learn how this course and the information provided impacted your view of worship.

1. What is your gender?
   a. Male
   b. Female

2. How old are you?
   a. 12-18
   b. 19-35
   c. 36-49
   d. 50-64
   e. 65+

3. How long have you attended worship at the Church of the Living God?
   - ☐ Less than one year
   - ☐ 1-3 years
   - ☐ 3-10 years
   - ☐ Over 10 years

4. How often do you typically attend worship at the Church of the Living God?
   - ☐ Every week
   - ☐ 2-3 times each month

☐ Once a month
☐ Only on holidays
☐ Sporadically
☐ Other (ex. Holidays, Funerals, Weddings)_____
_____

5. Do you have children living at home? YES NO
   a. If so, do they typically attend worship with you? YES NO
   b. What are their ages? _____

6. Which worship service do you primarily attend?
   ☐ Sunday at 10:15am
   ☐ Wednesday at 6:45pm

7. What is your CURRENT SATISFACTION with the worship service you primarily attend?
   ☐ Very Satisfied
   ☐ Somewhat Satisfied
   ☐ Neither Satisfied or Dissatisfied
   ☐ Somewhat Dissatisfied
   ☐ Very Dissatisfied

8. Which worship style do you MOST prefer?
   ☐ Traditional – Choir, Hymnals, use of the organ, use of liturgy such as responsive reading, creeds and Lord's Prayer
   ☐ Contemporary – Music on screen only, mostly praise music, use of guitar/drums, minimal use of liturgy.
   ☐ Blended – A mixture of both traditional and contemporary styles.
   ☐ Other _____

9. Which style of music do you MOST prefer in Corporate Worship at Shalom? (You may pick up to 2)
   ☐ Hymns
   ☐ Contemporary Gospel

- ❐ Traditional Gospel
- ❐ Christian Rap
- ❐ Christian Rock
- ❐ Praise and Worship
- ❐ None

10. Which style of music do you MOST prefer in your Private Worship time? (You may pick up to 2)
    - ❐ Hymns
    - ❐ Contemporary Gospel
    - ❐ Traditional Gospel
    - ❐ Christian Rap
    - ❐ Christian Rock
    - ❐ Praise and Worship
    - ❐ None

11. How many Music and Worship Appreciation Courses did you attend?
    - ❐ 1
    - ❐ 2
    - ❐ 3
    - ❐ 4

12. Do you feel that your assessment about worship has evolved?
    - ❐ Yes
    - ❐ No
    - ❐ Maybe

13. Are you open to receiving other expressions of worship in the current worship format of the church?
    - ❐ Yes
    - ❐ No
    - ❐ Maybe

14. Which styles of music in worship were you more engaged with when presented?
    a. Hymns
    b. Contemporary Gospel
    c. Traditional Gospel
    d. Christian Rap
    e. Christian Rock
    f. Praise and Worship
    g. None

Please share what you have learned from this course and how it has enhanced your view about worship. Be specific with your views before and after the course.

Music Worship Appreciation Four-Week Curriculum

WEEK 1

SURVEY
- Pass out Pre-Survey and give a minimum of 10 minutes to attendees to complete.

WORSHIP FORMAT – (Traditional Devotion)

> SCRIPTURE – Psalm 100
> PRAYER
> 2 SONG WORSHIP SET

Introduction of Myself and acknowledgements to Bishop Waddell and Volunteers

PURPOSE AND GOALS FOR THIS PROJECT

This seminar is research for me and the doctoral program I am completing. I believe that this project will be a blessing to this church. This project will last for four sessions. In most situations it can go as long as eight to ten weeks. However, we are going to pack as much as we can in four weeks. I am confident that each week will be power packed and prepare us to see something awesome take place in this ministry. This seminar will expose everyone who attends this church to a diversity of styles of worship. The intention behind it is to promote change and unity in the area of music and worship.

This area in most churches is always evolving and has become one of the most divisive components of the church. I will address that statement later. I am expecting that there will be diverse opinions. I welcome everyone's honest opinions. I am not expecting everyone to embrace every style that will be presented. However, by the end of these four weeks the desire is to create harmony between the different generations in this church and to make the worship here an inclusive experience for everyone here and those to come.

There will be tangible benefits that will come out of these sessions. Potential growth (numerically, statistically, financially, and spiritually) and changed lives for the glory of God will be the fruit of this program. Each week we will experience, discuss, engage, and learn together.

REFLECTION

- 15-minute discussion and analyzation about the worship just presented.

Let's reflect upon the worship we just experienced. This is something we will do each week. As we reflect, I am not asking for criticism or praise. I want us to asses by focusing our attention upon the music and the style of songs done in this session.

THE EVOLUTION OF WORSHIP IN A MINISTRY SETTING

"The way we traditionally expressed Christianity may be in trouble, but the future may hold new expressions of the Christian faith every bit as effective, faithful, meaningful, and world-transforming as those we've know so far."[212]

Worship is a vehicle and means that is evolving in the church. God uses worship to get closer to man. Culture has great influence on this evolution. In my experience, nothing in life of a church generates tension, anxiety, and conflict like change in worship.[213] However,

---

[212] Dan Kimball. *Emerging Worship: Creating Worship Gatherings for New Generations.* (Grand Rapids: Zondervan, 2004.) ix.

[213] Robb Redman. *The Great Worship Awakening: Singing a New Song in the Postmodern Church.* (San Francisco: Jossey-Bass, 2002.), xiii.

leaders must be conscious of the evolution and changes of culture. Perspectives, innovations, and styles of worship are being influenced and is worth discovery and assessment.

In Reggie McNeal's book, The Present Future, Six Tough Questions for the Church; he says, "the current church culture in North America is on life support."[214] In other words, he is saying that churches in this age are literally surviving and living off the hard work, money, and energy of previous generations. Therefore, there is an urgent need for some methodical changes because many churches are in denial.

It is visible that the politics and economics in North America is changing all around us. However, the missional effectiveness and worship lifestyles of the church are not. Most churches need to change because they're showing little to no statistical growth (numerical, spiritual, or otherwise) and minimal impact on the surrounding cultures. Generations are seeking refuge, salvation, and worship experiences that allow them to bring their evolving cultures, customs, and ways of life into churches that are holding onto "yesterday." Many of these churches have no awareness of the present things evolving around them for the fear of losing their principles.

Changing of methods does not mean erasing principles. However, learning what is best for the church requires prayer and courage so that worship will become fruitful for all generations in the life of the church. Fluidity with balance is crucial in how worship is approached in church. We should consider using innovative expressions to reach diverse groups in the church so that the Gospel is presented in a way that creates a response.

- Saying that, let's take about 15 minutes to answer this question. If you were to build the perfect worship service in church, what would it look like?

---

[214] Reggie McNeal. *Present Future: Six Tough Questions for the Church.* (Somerset: John Wiley & Sons, Inc.,2003.), 1.

THEOLOGY OF BIBLICAL WORSHIP

- Biblical Influences
  - o Old Testament worshippers did not have direct access to God. Our worship is forever more unencumbered by the law. Jesus was the fulfillment of the law and because of Him, the hole between God and mankind because of sin is gone. We presently have what no Old Testament worshiper ever had. We do not have to send burnt offerings to reach God. Jesus made it easy for us to touch and reach God. This is all the proof we need that Jesus is the Son of God. (Matt. 27:50-54) Worship changed forever when the veil in the Temple was torn...
  - o Our worship now has more understanding, reason, and purpose behind it. We worship a Holy Man that not only died, but also arose and is alive today. With His resurrection, He showed us and paved the way on how to go directly to God. The veil being ripped allows us to go directly to the throne room where God is. With His resurrection transpiring on a particular day and time of the year, Christians celebrate this event each year for Easter. We also worship on Sundays, which is different from the Jewish Custom. They still worship on the Sabbath.
- Cultural Influences
  - o The adaptation and influence of culture should not cause us to lose the critical and basic elements of the gospel because we are focusing so much on contextualization and begin to change our religious elements in order to adapt to culture. This is also called syncretism.
  - o Culture influences our freedom to express ourselves openly. Warren Bird said this in his book, 11 Innovations in the Local Church; "Our failure to impact

contemporary culture is not because we have not been relevant enough, but because we have not been real enough."

- Biblical Language of Worship
    - o I used to live in the East Coast for 10 years. Before I knew it, I began to start adopting to how they talk. The culture and the language became a part of my language and character. *"honor," "praise," "serve," "bow down," "sing," "clap," "shout"*

QUESTIONS

SURVEY

- Pass out Pre-Survey and consent to any new attendees to complete.

WORSHIP FORMAT – (Contemporary - Praise and Worship)

PRAYER

SCRIPTURE – PSALM 100

2 SONG WORSHIP SET

REFLECTION

- 15-minute discussion and analyzation about the worship just presented.

Let's reflect upon the worship we just experienced. This is something we will do each week. As we reflect, I am not asking for criticism or praise. I want us to asses by focusing our attention upon the music and the style of songs done in this session.

In this age, the battle of worship is very relevant. It is the battle between personal preferences, styles of music, liturgical interpretations, etc. These things have become the battleground and fallout in the Christian Church, hindering the focus on God being glorified and the people edified during worship services. In Genesis 3-4 there are some separate illustrations in which we can find "worship wars."

The first war is between *Satan and God*. Satan was conceited yet envious of God. His intimate relationship with God was tainted due to his rebellion, pride, and his heart filled with sin believing that he was better than God. In the present church, pride has overtaken the hearts of many. The desire to be worshipped rather than to worship God has become a major issue. This has been visible overtime in leadership. (Musicians, singers, preachers, and visible leadership.) Everyone wants to be worshipped.

The second worship war is *Satan vs. Mankind*. Satan was a

master of disguise. In Genesis, he used intimidation, eye-catching, and even in a harmless manner, disguised himself as a serpent in which Eve had dominion over. He was seductive and sneaky in order to get what he wanted. That was to make Eve lose what she had. What did she have? Her innocence. It was because of Eve's disobedience, although Satan manipulated her; there was an eternal price to be paid. "Everything changed, including man's worship. Where it once was natural and free, it was now inhibited because of mankind's altered physical proximity with God."[215] There are many examples that we could find in scripture and in present day circumstances. I talked about these to set the backdrop for what we are going to engage in today. Different styles of worship.

Many churches are daring to be different in ways they present the gospel. There are many innovative expressions being done in the church today to reach diverse groups of people. Cutting-edge methods of doing church like: *cyber-enhanced churches, community transforming churches, multi-site churches, ancient-future churches*, and so many more. Ways to change up how worship is done is not new. Change is necessary. Society is ever-changing. What we do today may not be good for tomorrow. Fluidity with balance is a crucial approach in church. We have to continue to find fresh methods to meet needs while maintaining biblical principles.

ANCIENT – FUTURE CHURCH

From our discussion last week, I concluded that the Ancient-Future Church style will be the best style for this ministry setting. In the Ancient-Future Church, it does not totally reject any particular style or structure of worship. A church using this method typically maintains a high view of Scripture. It adheres to the historic doctrines of faith and emphasize a transforming relationship with Jesus Christ. This style helps to keep the structure of religious belief as well as an understanding that man is flawed and have not completely figured out how to do church. Some elements that have

---

[215] Vernon M. Whaley. *Called to Worship: From the Dawn of Creation to the Final Amen.* (Nashville, TN: Thomas Nelson, 2009), 33.

been brought back into worship services are hymns and liturgy. They emphasize a shift in how worship is done. I am convinced that *the church can enthusiastically be ancient, future, and biblical all at the same time.*

The positive aspects of this type of worship is that it focuses on churchgoers and emerging generations of unchurched people. *Last week from our discussion it was stated that the worship format that included the song gave you all a connection to history, it was relative to your upbringing, had a richness and substance that you feel is invisible in the church currently.* I chose this method for this church because I believe that this model will help **hold on to yesterday for foundation while building today by reaching for what's ahead tomorrow.** Warren Bird said, "our failure to impact contemporary culture is not because we have not been relevant enough, but because we have not been real enough." Every element must focus and point worshipers to a genuine experience with Christ.

Just as there are positive aspects, there are also negative ones too this particular style. The negative aspects are the dangers of repeating the mindset and errors of faith from the past. In the book of Acts all kinds of corruption into the Church. Rituals can lead to error. If we put ritual over a surrendered heart, we will find ourselves in trouble. Let's customize this style of worship to fit this church by looking at two different worship models.

- Traditional vs. Contemporary Worship Models

Contemporary Worship

"The word *contemporary* is derived from the root words *con* and *tempus*, or "with the times."[216] This suggest that whatever is the "current style" of music could be considered contemporary. Another way of saying it, whatever is popular in church music today. This style or culture of music is driven by "popular culture" rather than "church culture." It is the music that we hear on the radios.

---

[216] Greg Scheer. *The Art of Worship: A Musician's Guide to Leading Modern Worship.* (Michigan: Baker Books, 2006), 12.

Most recognized, this style of worship can be more identified as a **Praise and Worship** musical genre. This is the style of musical worship that is practiced in most churches around the globe. A praise team or ensemble of singers render this genre of music during the worship service. The organ becomes obsolete while the guitar becomes the lead instrument in this musical presentation. Hymns begin to fade away and are after thoughts rather than priorities in the musical portion of worship. The use of power point, video presentations, lights, smoke, and other advanced technological and exciting features become a part of this particular worship model.

Although music plays a major role in model of worship, there are other components that change also. The terminologies have changed of how we define different parts of worship. For example: Invocation/Prayer, Sermon/Rendering of the Word) *In some situations worship services have turned into concert experiences.* But, the common goal in this style of worship is to use the things that are in current/popular culture to open the hearts of those attending worship.

Traditional Worship

This is the most common view of what church worship is. The structure of the worship experience has a choir, hymns, a preacher, pews, organ, and etc. This style would be considered the "old way of doing things." It is what our parents and grandparents grew up on. This style is beginning to become invisible in the church in this age.

According to the Strong's concordance, tradition is defined as *what has been handed down from one generation to the next.* This style of worship has the components of worship that can still be found in the archives of how the church order of worship has been established. This style isn't concerned about marketing, trying to "revitalize" the church, adapt to what is popular in music or culture, or letting go of what built the church in times past.

Music is still a driver in this style of service, but in a traditional sense. The Sermon is still the heart and central focus of the worship experience. This style of service is thematic in structure that is sermon-dominated. Every component of this "worship model serves the preaching."[217] The service goal is the sermon. All the music prepares, centers around, and summarize the theme of the sermon. Most mainline denominations like the Presbyterian, Methodist, Baptist, and Catholic churches use a more traditional influence in worship.

This style has not conformed to the Praise and Worship culture of this age. It remains true to what has been passed down historically. This type of service attracts and minister to a demographic of more elderly people. Leaving a huge weight on the sermon allowing the other components to always be one dimensional as a support to the individual's lead for that worship experience. These worship services historically do not attract many youth because the musical component of worship is not likely the preference of younger generations.

Question: Which out of these 2 models do you think will be the most effective in this church? **In my opinion, both!**

Blended Worship Model

"The more common term for convergence worship, especially as it relates to musical styles, is *blended* worship."[218] Most blended worships aren't done very well due to theological ignorance. Blended worship is a mixture of **Historic**, **Traditional** also known as **Thematic**, **Contemporary** also known as **Experiential**, and **Global** expressions worship models. However, they don't always turn out successful. The challenges usually evolve around which elements should be kept and which parts to bring over into worship.

There are four-parts in the worship structure that must remain consistent. They are: **Gathering, Word, Table, and Dismissal.** The intent for blended worship is to find common ground so that all demographics will be ministered too. Being able to bridge the gap between tradition and contemporary. Bridging the gap between the elderly and the youth is the central goal for blended worship.

---

[217] Ibid, 91.

[218] Ibid, 97.

Blended worship is a formula that has an intentional goal just as the Contemporary and Traditional forms do. That goal is to *bring glory to God* and to bring man closer to God. This style of worship can be looked as a new and improved style of worship. It mixes instrumentation, hymns, praise and worship, and eliminates some of the traditional liturgy and worship practices so that the total man is being edified and God glorified.

HOMEWORK ASSIGNMENT - What elements in worship of this church do you think we should keep, and which should be altered?

QUESTIONS

WORSHIP FORMAT – (Traditional - Hymns)

PRAYER
SCRIPTURE – PSALM 100
2 SONG WORSHIP SET

REFLECTION
- 15-minute discussion and analyzation about the worship just presented.

Let's reflect upon the worship we just experienced. This is something we will do each week. As we reflect, I am not asking for criticism or praise. I want us to asses by focusing our attention upon the music and the style of songs done in this session.

DEMOGRAPHIC SURVEY

RACE/ETHNICITY

Caucasian	61.3%
Black	28.6%
Hispanic	2.7%
Asian	3.6%
Other	3.0%

GENDER

Males	46.8% = 7,901
Females	53.2% - 9,000

AGE
The median age of residents is 41 years old.

CRIME RATE
Below the national average per 100,000 people.

INCOME LEVEL PER HOUSEHOLD (DEFINE LOCAL DATA INCOME RANGES)
Estimated median household income is $62,489. (2016)

EDUCATION LEVELS

HS/GED	92.4%
Bachelors	31.8%
Graduate or Professional	14.5%

RELATIONSHIP STATUS

Never Married	31.6%
Now Married	49.1%
Separated	2.7%
Widowed	5.7%
Divorced	10.9%

FAITH TRADITIONS BEYOND CHRISTIANITY

Catholic	17.2%
Evangelical Protestant	17.4%
Orthodox	.8%
Black Protestant	3.8%
Mainline Protestant	9.1%
Other	2.2%
None	**49.6%**[219]

COTLG is 99.9% predominately African American. There has always been a divide in most churches, a disconnect between races,

---

[219] "City-Data.com - Stats about all US cities - real estate, relocation info, crime, house prices, cost of living, races, home value estimator, recent sales, income, photos, schools, maps, weather, neighborhoods, and more." City-Data.com - Stats about all US cities - real estate, relocation info, crime, house prices, cost of living, races, home value estimator, recent sales, income, photos, schools, maps, weather, neighborhoods, and more. Accessed May 21, 2018. http://www.city-data.com/.

generations, cultures, and ethnicities.[220] The statistics that I provided show that COTLG will benefit from expanding its reach. This will draw more members from a wider community. This does not mean that the inner community should be neglected. It shows that the reach of the church should reach beyond "Jerusalem." The data compiled also shows that COTLG may benefit by considering being open to a multi-racial worship style in this community. But since we do not rely on the inner community as a part of the congregation, we must look at some ways to influence surrounding cultures and generations.

WHAT ARE SOME MUSICAL INFLUENCES IN THE CHURCH?
- **Sacred music** is one of three expressions of European classical **music**, which also includes chamber **music** and theater **music**. **Sacred music** is, simply put, **music** written for church. Sacred Music Influences – hymns, gospel, quartet, choir – Thomas Dorsey, Mahalia Jackson…etc.
- **Secular music** is any **music** not written for the church. The earliest written **secular** songs, the Goliard Songs were poems about women, wine, and satire and were notated in a manner that we still cannot fully decipher. Secular Music Influences – Pop, Rock, Folk

A CULTURALLY INFLUENCED WORSHIP
- Creates greater harmony and unity amongst the membership as it learns to appreciate the diverse ways we worship individually and corporately.
- The churches that grow the most are the ones who invest two areas. These two areas of importance in the church to provide balance and focus in *ecclesiology* and *missiology*. Ecclesiology ("study of church") helps us to understand what a church is and how it should function. Missiology ("study of mission") helps us to see what methods and ministries

---

[220] Soong – Chan Rah. *Many Colors: Cultural Intelligence for a Changing Church.* (Chicago: Moody Publishers, 2010), 52.

will be most effective at reaching our community. Although change is constant, the circumstances of change differ from generation to generation. The way we do and think about church is very valid!

- An important component about this is that the church knows its DNA and stick with it!

MISSING GENERATIONS IN THE CHURCH
- **The Silent Generation:** Born 1928-1945 (73-90 years old)
- **Baby Boomers:** Born 1946-1964 (54-72 years old)
- **Generation X:** Born 1965-1980 (38-53 years old)
- **Millennials:** Born 1981-1996 (22-37 years old)
- **Post-Millennials:** Born 1997-Present (0-21 years old)

The ages from 18 – 35 years old are coming up missing in the church because the culture in our communities and in the world has shifted. The youth that are in the churches now are those who more than likely grew up in the church. The ones that have not grown up in church are saying that church doesn't fit them. There is a greater percentage of millennials deciding not to come back into church for several reasons that begin with the style issues in worship. Leaders are not effectively embracing the needs of this generation. The worship services are simply repeating itself in churches without embracing change or being open minded to rethink how they do church to win the lost generations. Saying that, last week I gave a homework assignment. This week we were going to assess...

HOMEWORK ASSIGNMENT - What elements in worship of this church do you think we should keep, and which can be altered?

BENEFITS OF CREATING AN INCLUSIVE AND CULTURALLY SENSITIVE WORSHIP FORMAT
It is important to know that God continues to seek us out of His desire to be closer with us. That is an amazing thought. **God pursuits us! And He repeatedly pursuits us...He continues to pursuit us...an**

eternal and non-stop desire. *It is a passionate pursuit that transcends time, culture, place, and any restriction.* If He does it, we must be continuously open to doing the same by creating more opportunities for believers and unbelievers to get close to God.

- Personal Benefit
- Corporate Benefit

QUESTIONS

WORSHIP FORMAT – (Blended Worship)

THE GATHERING

Call to Worship   *Worship Leader*

   Responsive Reading   *Psalm 100*
   Prayer of Invocation

Congregational Worship   **Worship Team** – *How Great is Our God, For Your Glory, Shine on Me*

Family Prayer
   The Lord's Prayer

Welcome   *Welcome Ministry – (Mother/Youth)*

Worship through Music   *Music Ministry*

Message from the Lord   *Chief Bishop Rex Waddell*

Invitation to Life

Worship through Giving   *(Media Presentation) – Worship Leader*

Announcements   *Media Ministry*

Benediction   *Worship Leader*

REFLECTION

- 15-minute discussion and analyzation about the worship just presented.

Let's reflect upon the worship we just experienced. This is something we will do each week. As we reflect, I am not asking for criticism or praise. I want us to asses by focusing our attention upon the music and the style of songs done in this session.

WHERE DO WE GO FROM HERE?

The success and effectiveness of this worship strategy can only come through a unified community that integrates and collaborates with each other to propel growth in an efficient and effective way. John Maxwell said, "Leadership is not about titles, positions or flowcharts. It is about one life influencing another." We cannot make a difference in the kingdom of God without influencing one another. There is no "I" on the Lord's team. It is essential that we, "develop a structure that honor integration." "We must look for the common good of the ministry by utilizing the various gifts in the house and empowering our people as one body and one church."

Worship is an action word. Worship is not an event. It is a lifestyle choice. It is a vehicle and means that God used as a way to get closer to humanity. Worship is expressed through our preaching, singing, fellowship, prayer, breaking of bread, spontaneous praise, and celebration. Everything in our life begins to transform in the atmosphere of worship. Worship shows our position and place in God. Worship does more for us than it does for God.

Whether private or corporate worship, we are nurtured, and God is glorified. There is nothing wrong with using the Old Testament traditions we have grown up on as long as the purpose and mindset of each worship experience has a New Testament method and theme. **Psalm 145:1-4**

I will exalt you, my God the King;
I will praise your name for ever and ever.
Every day I will praise you
and extol your name for ever and ever.
Great is the Lord and most worthy of praise;
his greatness no one can fathom.
One generation commends your works to another;
they tell of your mighty acts.

Let's take a moment to Worship and thank God for what we shared these few weeks…

I have so much more to share, but no more time. I pray that these sessions will have some influence in the possibilities in this church and in your personal life.

QUESTIONS

POST SURVEY

DR. TIMOTHY D. PRICE, III

afterthis314@gmail.com
LinkedIn: https://www.linkedin.com/in/timothy-price-iii-9b88a111b
Blog: www.theehealingplace.com.wordpress.com

Curriculum Vitae

EDUCATION

South University, Savannah, GA
School of Ministry
Doctoral of Ministry, December 2016 – November 2019
    DMin Final Project: "Assessing Cultural Influences in Worship"

Liberty University, Lynchburg, VA
School of Music
M.A. in Worship Studies with Cognate in Leadership, July 2015 - February 2017

Liberty University, Lynchburg, VA
School of Religion
B.S. in Religion, February 2013 - May 2015

RESEARCH AND TEACHING INTERESTS

Pastoral Studies; Religion; Communications; Leadership; Sacred Music; Worship Studies; Evangelism

PERSONAL SKILLS

- **Administrative skills:** Type at least 55wpm, Data Entry, proficient in all clerical duties, timely, organized, and strong attention to detail.

- **Management:** Self-motivated and specializes in the area of ministry development which includes: hiring, leadership development, budget and revenue management, quality assurance, policy and procedure implementation, fundraisers, etc.
- Accomplished Pianist/Organist/Singer/Conductor with a broad range of musical styles.
- Skilled teacher in various areas such as choirs, ensembles, bands, leadership development, preaching, and teaching biblical studies.
- Able to prepare curriculum and manuals for small groups, churches, and classes.
- Experience with studio and live productions.

PROFESSIONAL MUSICAL EXPERIENCE

<u>Musical Recordings</u>

- GMWA Youth Department (Higher Ground Recording Label)
- Gateway Area Chapter (Too King Records)
- Timothy Price and Vision (Too King Records)
- Life and Times of Malcolm X (Maestro Anthony Davis and NYC Symphony Orchestra) – Young Malcolm Little
- Live in Japan – "I Found It"
- Bishop Shelton Bady and the Voices of Harvest along with Timothy Price (Live)
- Bethel AME Christmas CD (Baltimore Sun and Macy's collaboration)
- Transform Me (Bethel AME Gospel Hip Hop CD)
- Timothy Price and Destiny (Fresh Fire International)
- Rodney Bryant (Tyscot Recording Label)
- A Psalmist Heart (Independent)
- Next Generation Choir (City of Peace Record Label)
- Dr. F. James Clark Presents Shalom Church and Friends (City of Peace Record Label)

<u>Television Appearances:</u>

- Fox News – St. Louis, MO
- TBN Praise the Lord - Houston, TX
- Daystar - Houston, TX

<u>Stage Appearances:</u>

- Tour in Japan - Nagoya, Tokyo, Toyota
- London - Concert w Min. Stephen Hurd
- New York Production - "Life and Times of Malcolm X"
- The Muny Opera - "Porgy and Bess"
- The Fox Theatre - "The Nutcracker"
- Houston Black Rep. Theatre - "Crowns"

<u>Artists performed with:</u>

Min. Stephen Hurd, Pattie LaBelle, Fantasia, Kelly Price, Rodney Bryant, Maurette Brown-Clark, The Oneal Twins, Maestro Anthony Davis, New York Chamber Orchestra, Dello Thedford, Donnie McClurkin, and more.

PROFESSIONAL MINISTERIAL EXPERIENCE

Shalom Church City of Peace   St. Louis, MO
   Music Administrator/Organist/
   Adjunct Director
Temple Church of Christ, Apostolic   St. Louis, MO
   Organist and Worship Leader
Bethel AME Church   Baltimore, MD
   Minister of Music
Harvest Time Church   Houston, TX
   Director of Fine Arts

Mt. Zion Baptist Church   Woodlawn, OH
    Organist and Worship Leader
Temple of Judah   St. Louis, MO
    Senior Pastor
Mt. Sinai Baptist Church   Mt. Holly, NC
    Minister of Music

PUBLICATIONS AND PUBLICATIONS IN PREPARATION

"The Importance of Your Praise and Worship", 1998 *Manual AUR*
"Philosophy of Praise and Worship, 2002 *Manual AUR*
"Relationship" *Pastor and Musician (Do You Have It)*, 2003 *Manual AUR*
"The Full Circle of Music in the Church", 2005 *Manual AUR*
"The Next Dimension," *A Quick Study for the Ready to be Inspired Artist*, www.lulu.com,2006
"Provoking Thoughts" *Poetry Book*, www.lulu.com,2006
"After This" www.lulu.com, 2015
"Sunday Morning Appetizers," *forthcoming*
"30 Days of Renewal", *forthcoming*
Word and Music Blog, *active*, www.theehealingplace.wordpress.com
"Accessing Cultural Influences in Worship," 2019

HONORS AND AWARDS

COGIC Eastern Missouri First Jurisdiction – Bishop Robert J. Ward Leadership Award, 2017
The Watson and Williams Educational Scholarship, 2017
The Baltimore Sun Gospel Choir Competition Winner, 2006
Rodgers Organ Scholarship, 2004, 2005
Induction into the National Honor's Society for Theology Students

PROFESSIONAL MEMBERSHIPS

Gospel Music Workshop of America
National Convention of Gospel Choirs and Choruses
Theta Alpha Kappa
National Funeral Directors Association

RELIGIOUS AFFILIATIONS

Church of God in Christ Incorporated
American Baptist
Pentecostal Assemblies of the World

SERVICE TO THE PROFESSION

Panelist for Black History Symposium NCGCC Gospel Archive Project
Workshop Clinician and Ministry Consultant for "Kingdom Growth and Church Expansion Strategies"

REFERENCES ARE AVAILABLE UPON REQUEST

Printed in the United States
By Bookmasters